MICHAEL W. PITTS

LATER STONE IMPLEMENTS

SHIRE ARCHAEOLOGY

TITLES IN THE SHIRE ARCHAEOLOGY SERIES
with their series numbers

Anglo-Saxon Jewellery Ronald Jessup (1)
Anglo-Saxon Pottery David H. Kennett (5)
Barrows in England and Wales Leslie V. Grinsell (8)
Bronze Age Metalwork in England and Wales Nancy G. Langmaid (4)
Flint Implements of the Old Stone Age Peter Timms (2)
Later Stone Implements Michael W. Pitts (14)
Medieval Pottery in Britain Jeremy Haslam (6)
Pottery in Roman Britain Vivien G. Swan (3)
Prehistoric Pottery Nancy G. Langmaid (7)
Prehistoric Stone Circles Aubrey Burl (9)
Roman Coinage in Britain P. J. Casey (12)
Roman Roads Richard W. Bagshawe (10)
Roman Villas David E. Johnston (11)
Towns in Roman Britain Julian Bennett (13)

Published by
SHIRE PUBLICATIONS LTD
Cromwell House, Church Street, Princes Risborough,
Aylesbury, Bucks, HP17 9AJ, UK.

Series Editor: James Dyer

ISBN 0 85263 518 4

First published 1980

Printed in Great Britain by
C. I. Thomas & Sons (Haverfordwest) Ltd,
Press Buildings, Merlins Bridge, Haverfordwest.

Contents

1. INTRODUCTION 5
2. RAW MATERIALS 7
3. MANUFACTURE 19
4. DISTRIBUTION 31
5. USE 37
6. CHANGE 45
7. WHAT CAN YOU DO? 50
GLOSSARY 51
BIBLIOGRAPHY 52
INDEX 55

Cover illustration
Arrowheads from Scotland, made from a variety of coloured stones. Clockwise from top right:
Culbin, Grampian (flint);
Eigg, Inner Hebrides, Highland (bloodstone);
Premnay, Grampian (flint);
Buchan, Grampian (flint);
Corriegills, Arran, Strathclyde (pitchstone);
Shapinsay, Orkney (flint);
Haremoss, Borders (porcellanite);
Centre: Stevenston, Strathclyde (quartz).
(Photograph: National Museum of Antiquities of Scotland.)

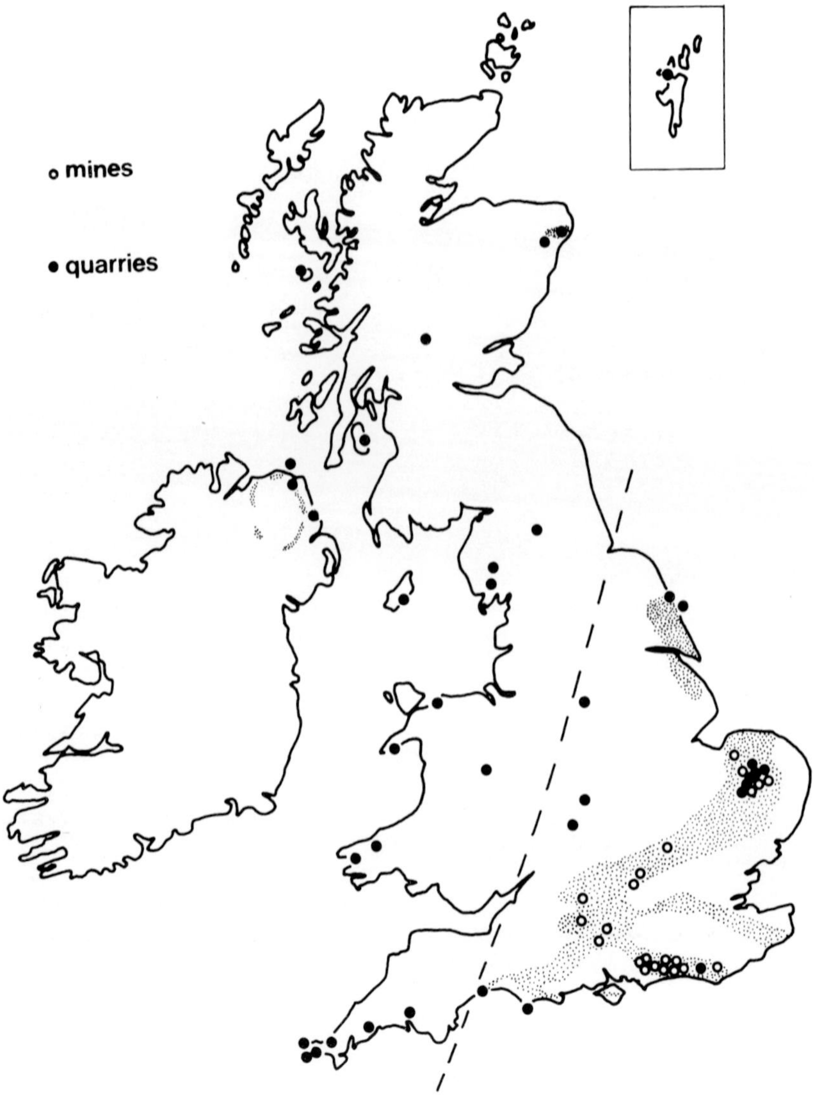

1. Location of known prehistoric mines and quarries. The mines, all into chalk, have tunnels excavated out of the rock. At quarries stone was procured by working exposures or by digging shallow pits. The main areas of chalk from which fresh flint could have been obtained are indicated by the shading. The dashed line is a rough divider between the parts of Britain where fresh flint was freely available (to the south-east) and those where it was harder to acquire (to the north-west).

1
Introduction

'In the following pages I purpose to give an account of the various forms of stone implements, weapons, and ornaments of remote antiquity discovered in Great Britain, their probable uses and method of manufacture, and also, in some instances, the circumstances of their discovery.' With these words Sir John Evans opened his massive work on prehistoric stone implements (listed in the bibliography), which to this day lies unrivalled. The aims of the following investigation of later stone tools are not intended to emulate those of Sir John. Such an 'account', presented today, would be misleading and based on assumptions of doubtful validity. I aim instead to explore the sort of questions which are being asked and which should be asked of prehistoric lithic material, in order to attain a true advance in knowledge.

For many years archaeologists have assumed that examination of the shape and size of any ancient stone artefact yielded all the information necessary for identification of its function. It has only recently been realised that in order fully to understand stone tools and the part they played in the life of prehistoric man it is imperative to understand the technology implicit in their production.

As stoneworking is today a rarely practised art, ethnography has been of limited assistance, and technological understanding has had to be gained chiefly through experimental work. Archaeologists themselves have had to learn to knap. As more and more begin to acquire the sensitive skills of stoneworking, it is becoming increasingly apparent that all over the prehistoric world technological accomplishments of a very high order were being achieved, for long unappreciated because of their irrelevance to our own technologies. Sophisticated skills are being rediscovered after thousands of years of total absence.

It is inevitable that a growing understanding of knapping technology should be accompanied by a parallel growth in technical vocabulary. Explicit descriptions of complicated processes demand a special language. What to me is an amorphous tangle under the bonnet of my car called an engine is to a motor mechanic an assemblage of parts, every one of which has an important and specific function. The mechanic's ability to name each one of these parts is vital to his understanding of the whole. In the same way all individual aspects of stoneworking require precise definition, as the miners at

Brandon who supplied the gun-flint industry fully appreciated. They dug sloping shafts in the chalk with alternately orientated rectangular stages. The slope was to protect the worker from the weather and falling stones. As one man said: 'I never sink stunt, but under-run my two by bubber-hutching on the sosh'. He could not have put it more precisely!

In a science where advances are being made so fast it is not surprising to find that no universally accepted terminology for describing worked stone exists. However, there are a number of basic words that have long become standard, and I have used some of these in the text. Their first appearance is italicised. It is important that these words are not used loosely.

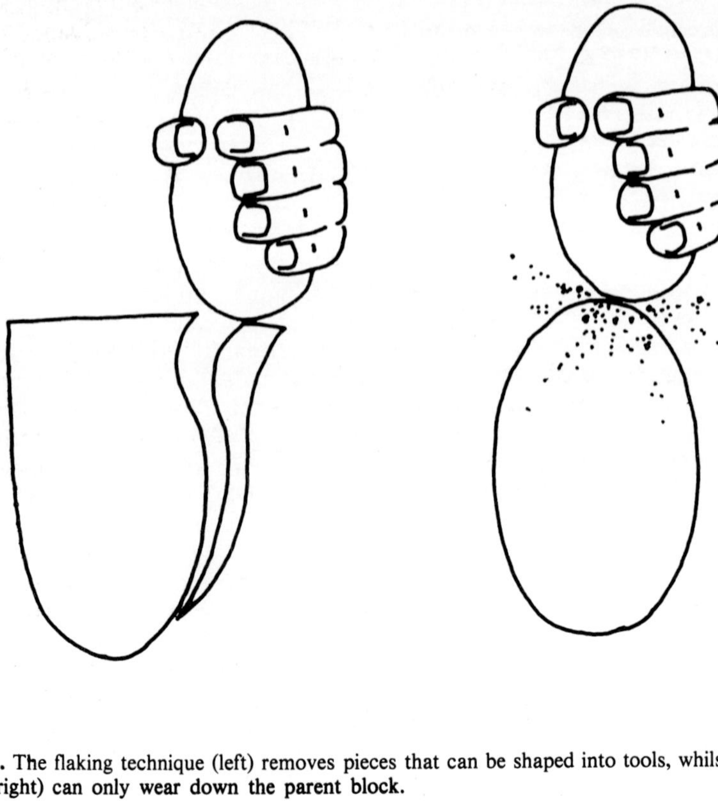

2. The flaking technique (left) removes pieces that can be shaped into tools, whilst pecking (right) can only wear down the parent block.

2
Raw materials

For most of us, the idea of working stone suggests carving. But throughout prehistory this was just about the only technique that was *not* used! The way people worked stone depended partly on the equipment they had available for the task, partly on what they hoped to make and, given these restrictions, the raw materials at their disposal. The predominant method used in prehistoric Britain – and throughout the world, for that matter – was flaking, by which technique *flakes* or chips were removed from a larger piece of stone with a hammer or pressure tool. The main requirements of stone for working in this way are that it should be even-textured, free of flaws, cracks, inclusions or natural cleavage planes, capable of withstanding a certain degree of shock, and should exhibit what is known as a *conchoidal fracture habit* without the application of excessive force (the main reason for the last restriction is that it is very difficult to control what you are doing if you have to muster all your energy into delivering a massive blow!). The possession of a conchoidal fracture habit means, in practice, that the stone when struck will not simply shatter or snap (or not break at all), but will fracture in a characteristic way immediately below the point of impact. If this point is near the edge of the piece, a flake will be removed. It is the predictability of this result that was so important to the stoneworker.

Frequently, however, we have evidence of the exploitation of stone types without the conchoidal fracture habit. These were principally igneous or metamorphic rocks in which the constituent minerals are readily crushed, but which nonetheless possess sufficient toughness and resilience to withstand continuous percussion. Such stone can be worked by pounding, hammering or *pecking*. Because the stone removed from the piece being struck in this process consists of little more than dust, it is only the parent lump that can be made into a tool, and not, as with flaking, the removals as well (fig. 1). Thus we find that implements made in this way are invariably large – usually axeheads – and that the small tools possible with flaking cannot be produced. Hard, igneous rock can however readily be drilled, whereas those stones suitable for flaking do not respond favourably to this technique. Drilling flint, for example, tends to generate a series of conchoidal fractures which cause the piece to break across the point of perforation.

As can be seen from the table (page 8), a great many types of

rock type	**working method**	
	predominantly flaking	*predominantly pecking*
silica	quartz chert flint bloodstone chalcedony carnelian agate jasper opal	
igneous	pitchstone rhyolite basalt augite granophyre (VII) riebeckite felsite (XXII) tuffs (VI, VIII, VIIIa, XI)	gabbro, epidiorite or greenstone (I, Ia, II, IIa, III, IIIa, XVI, XVII) sheared greenstone (IVa) picrite (XII) altered picrite (IV) granodiorite (XXIIIa) dolerite (XIII, XXIIIb) quartz dolerite (XVIII) altered quartz diorite (XXV) camptonite (XIV) granite porphyrites
metamorphic	porcellanite (IX) calc-silicate hornfels (XXIV, V) baked shale (XXI) quartzites amphibolite schistose grit epidotised ashy grit (XX) schists	quartzites
sedimentary	silicified sandstone mudstone siltstone shale clay ironstone clay slate sandstones	greywacke (XIX) micaceous sub-greywacke (XV)

Stone types used for making edge tools in prehistoric Britain. Roman numerals are Implement Petrology Group Numbers.

stone were worked in prehistoric Britain. Of these, flint, a fine form of chert found principally in the chalk of south and east England, was by far the most important in terms of quantity of tools produced. Flint exhibits good conchoidal fracture, is extremely hard and can take a razor-sharp edge: it is thus suitable for a wide range of implement types. However, over much of Britain good flint was locally unobtainable, and stones of other kinds had to be used for most purposes. It is possible to divide the British mainland into two zones: one where the locally available stone was predominantly fresh flint, and the other where derived flint (from beach or river gravels) and a range of non-flint materials (some more suited to the pecking technique) met the local demand.

It is often assumed that, exceptions apart, stone was obtained from surface exposures by simply picking it up off the ground. But it is much more likely that this form of winning was exceptional. Any flint on the surface would have been rendered difficult to work by the effects of the weather (especially freezing). In areas where flint did occur below the ground, it is likely that people would have dug for it. In the neolithic, construction of the many communal earthworks on the chalk would have led incidentally to much good flint being exposed, but in the mesolithic, a period from which large excavations of any kind are unknown, such a source can be discounted. How the hunter-gatherers obtained their flint, frequently of very high quality, is a mystery.

The igneous rocks used in antiquity were sometimes quarried from below ground, but evidence also exists for outcrop exploitation. As many of these rocks have very limited occurrences, it has been possible to isolate a number of sources and identify some of their products. In the early 1920s the petrographer to His Majesty's Geological Survey, Dr H. H. Thomas, was able to locate a source in south-west Wales for the igneous stones at Stonehenge by examining thin slices of rock under the microscope. In 1936 two ground axes from this same source were recognised from Ireland, and it was not long before the technique of thin-sectioning was being applied to the many stone axeheads from all over Britain. Since then, thousands of these axes have been sliced and, at the present count, twenty-five sources identified, each allocated a Petrological Group Number in Roman numerals. Most of the rocks examined were worked by pecking, so that one would not expect to find shaping debris at the sources. In some cases, however, the stones were flaked, and here vast quantities of quarry waste betray the exact sites exploited. Perhaps the two best known of these were at Scafell and Langdale Pikes in the Lake District and in the Penmaenmawr area in North Wales (assigned

3. Some of the hollows at Grime's Graves, Norfolk, that represent backfilled neolithic mine shafts in the chalk. The site is under the guardianship of the Department of the Environment, and a recently re-excavated shaft can be explored.

Petrological Group Numbers VI and VII respectively). Walking through the mists that frequently envelop these moorland sites, crunching underfoot the flakes and rubble that blanket the quarry areas, one might almost hear on the wind the steady tap-tap-tap of a neolithic stoneworker's hammer. The quantity of axes traced to these quarries alone is now approaching one thousand.

Much more impressive in terms of engineering achievement and sheer effort, however, are the mines excavated into the chalk of southern England in the quest for flint of high quality. Flint occurs in thin seams, in the form of tabular sheets or of isolated lumps called nodules. It seems that some of the best flint for knapping could only be obtained by digging deep into the chalk for these seams. Some twenty mine complexes have been found, although archaeologists suspect that more remain undiscovered. Radiocarbon determinations from some of these sites indicate that mining was in process throughout the neolithic, and the distribution of centres suggests exploitation of flint seams wherever suitable opportunities existed in the south. To date, however, no mines have been found north of East Anglia.

Circular shafts were sunk into the chalk, and when the desired flint seam was reached narrow galleries were tunnelled out to increase the return. A typical full-size shaft might be 6 metres (20 feet) in diameter and 8 metres (26 feet) deep. At each of the three largest mining centres, Cissbury near Brighton, Easton Down on the Wiltshire-Hampshire border and Grime's Graves on the Norfolk-Suffolk border, between two hundred and fifty and three hundred shafts are visible as saucer-shaped hollows, and many more undoubtedly lie hidden. The shafts are not open because of the way work was carried out: only one seems to have been in use at a time, and the chalk spoil from a new shaft was dumped into its freshly abandoned neighbour.

As with all similar engineering projects in the neolithic, these mines were excavated principally with tools of red deer antler. Although these are usually called 'picks', the nearest equivalent in use today is a crowbar. A projecting tine on the antler was hammered into the chalk, and blocks of rock were levered out with the long beam. A nearly identical tool (though made of iron and wood) was in use by gun-flint miners in East Anglia until the demise of the craft in the 1920s. Remarkably, one of the Sussex mine groups was discovered in about 1890 by a shepherd setting out hurdles for his flock. Working on the same principle as the antler 'picks', a crowbar was being used to hollow out footings for the hurdles. The shepherd saw two of his bars disappear through his fingers into the depths of the earth before a belated enquiry revealed him to be sited over some neolithic mine shafts.

It is frequently argued that neolithic flint mines served exclusively as axe production centres. This reasoning is based on the large quantities of irregular *bifaces* (flattish pieces with flakes removed from both faces) discovered during excavation of the mines. These bifaces are widely believed to represent *preforms*, that is intermediate stages in the production of finished retouched tools. The argument may be dismissed for two reasons. Firstly, these 'roughouts' are too rough to be preforms for anything; and secondly study of *all* the material from the mines, especially the waste, indicates that a wide range of tools and large cores were being made and removed for use elsewhere. In other words, the mines were sources of flint, not of axes.

In view of the success achieved in relating particular implements of

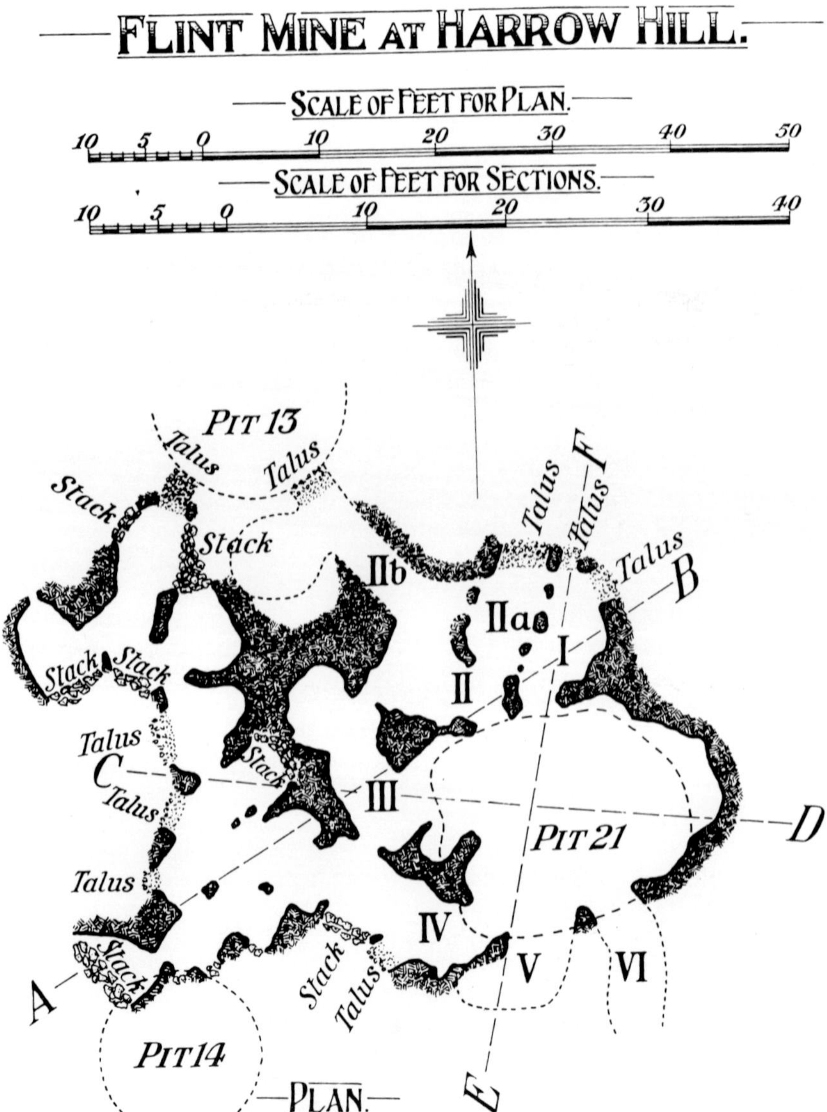

4. Plan and sections, drawn by Robert Gurd, of one of 160 visible neolithic mine shafts on Harrow Hill, near Worthing, West Sussex. This shaft was excavated between March 1924 and May 1925 by amateur archaeologists working mainly on Saturday afternoons. It would be most unwise to attempt similar work without the assistance of modern miners: several rock falls occurred in the 1920s excavations, although, somewhat miraculously, no one was hurt! (By permission of the Sussex Archaeological Society.)

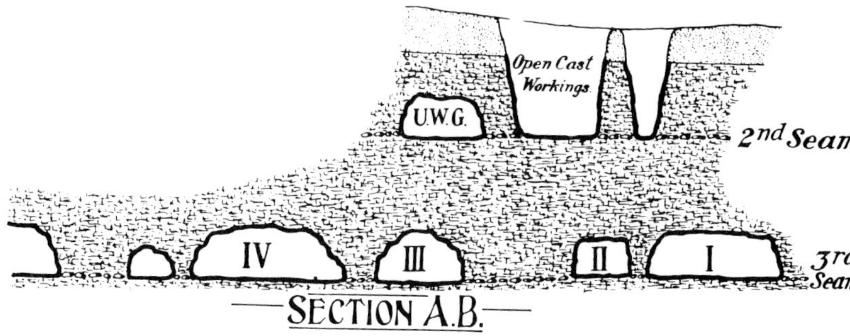
Open Cast Workings
U.W.G.
2nd Seam
IV
III
II
I
3rd Seam
SECTION A.B.

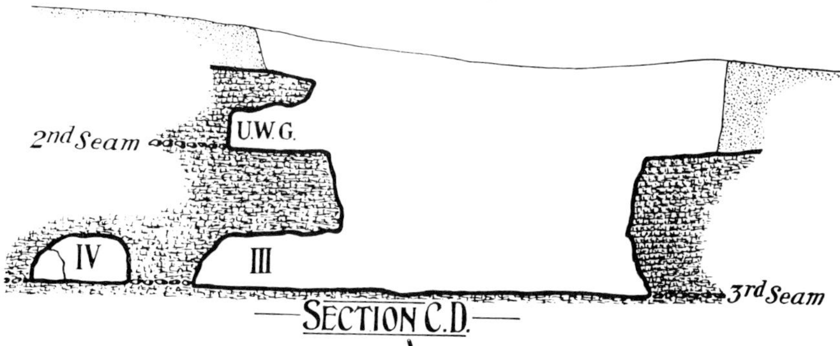
2nd Seam
U.W.G.
IV
III
3rd Seam
SECTION C.D.

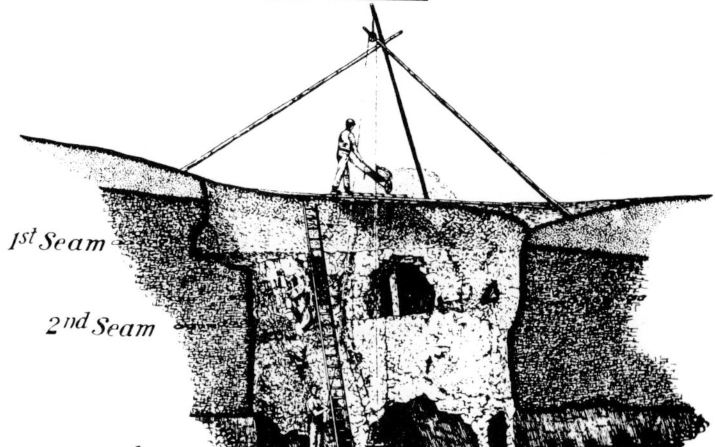
1st Seam
2nd Seam
3rd Seam
SECTION E.F.

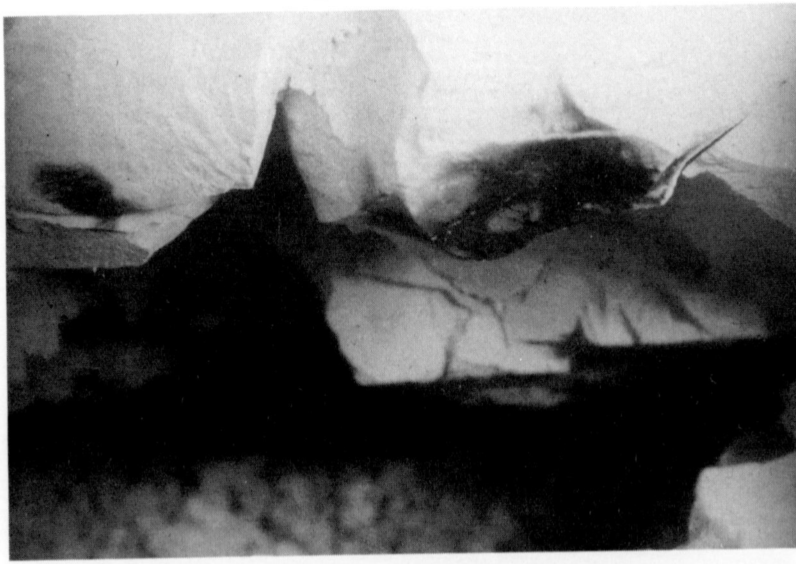

5. Soot marks from a miner's lamp on the roof of a gallery that radiated from the mine shaft at Harrow Hill. (Photograph: Sussex Archaeological Society.)
6. Holes in the wall of a gallery at Harrow Hill made with an antler 'pick'. This photograph and fig. 5 were taken in 1925. (Photograph: Sussex Archaeological Society.)

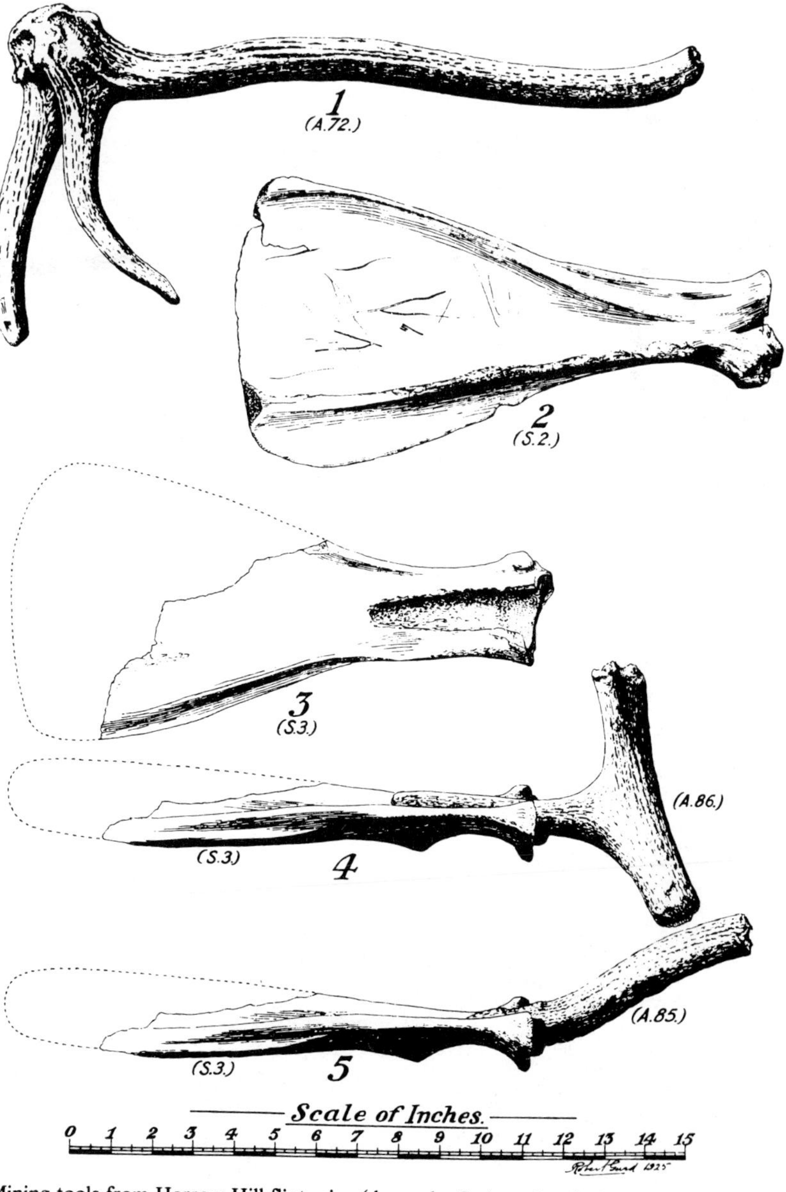

7. Mining tools from Harrow Hill flint mine (drawn by Robert Gurd). (By permission of the Sussex Archaeological Society.)

8. Pitchstone, a black glassy rock found on the Isle of Arran. It occurs freely on the surface and was used for flake tools in Scotland throughout prehistory.

igneous and metamorphic material to their sources, it has long been hoped that some method would be developed for characterising flint. It is frequently possible to identify a range of different flint types by colour among the tools and waste from a single settlement, but it is impossible within the present state of knowledge to suggest other than a probable local origin for most of these types. Most rocks can be readily characterised in thin section by their distinctive mineralogical composition, but flint, consisting almost entirely of pure silica, is not amenable to such an approach. Some recent analytical work, however, has shown that the trace-element content of flint varies from place to place, so that it should be possible in the near future to suggest general source areas. However, because the elemental variation is gradual and rather subtle, it seems that it will be feasible only to identify movement of pieces over large distances and not locally. For example, the flint of the South Downs can be distinguished from East Anglian chert by the relative amounts of aluminium and potassium; but it is not possible to distinguish between two mine centres in Sussex. Unfortunately, the analytical method is unsuited to small items, thus work in the immediate future is likely to centre on flint axes. The opportunity thus now seems to exist for recognising and mapping the occurrence of large-scale movement of axes from flint sources, analogous to the distribution of axes from some of the other stone quarries, if such movement existed. This is indeed an exciting prospect.

We cannot conclude this consideration of raw materials without a mention of jade. 'Jade' is a general term used to encompass a broad group of greenish igneous and metamorphic rocks. The hundred jade axes which have so far been found in Britain can be classified into three distinct mineralogical groups, jadeite, omphacite and rarely nephrite. Although no source areas have yet been positively identified, all jade axes are likely to have been imported from continental Europe.

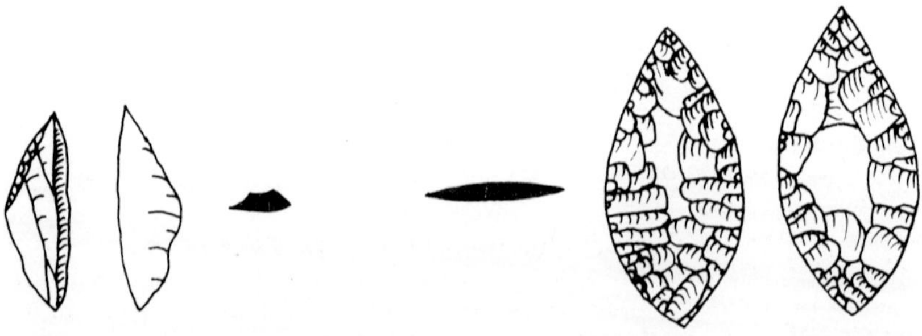

9. This mesolithic arrow point or barb (left) was made from a segment of a blade, whilst the neolithic arrowhead (right) was made from a wider and flatter flake (see fig. 11).

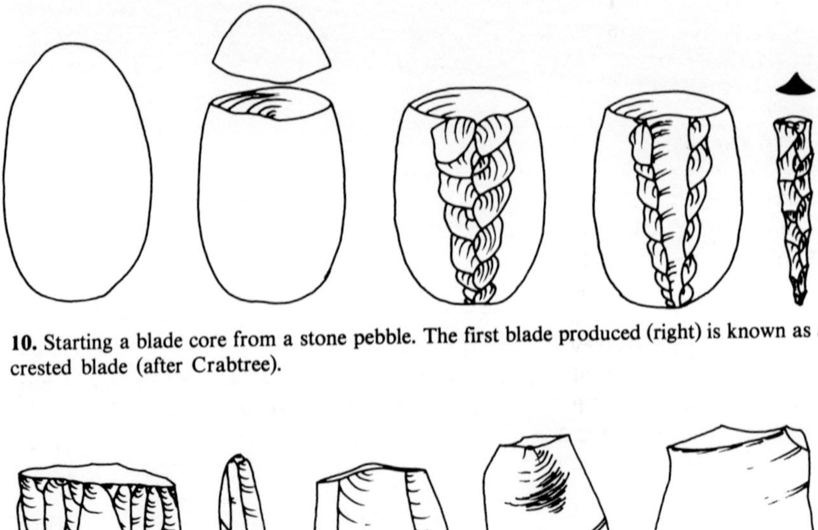

10. Starting a blade core from a stone pebble. The first blade produced (right) is known as a crested blade (after Crabtree).

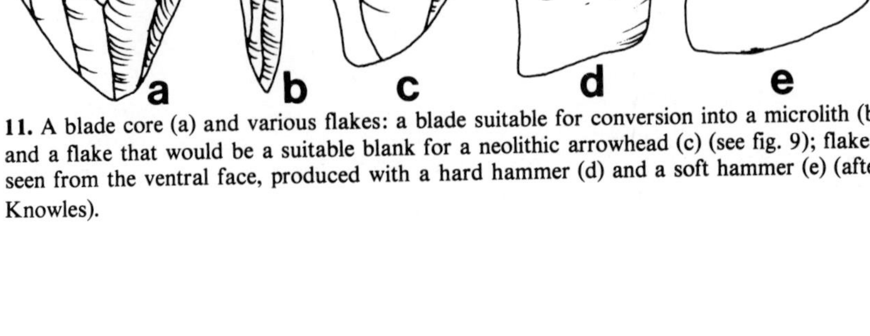

11. A blade core (a) and various flakes: a blade suitable for conversion into a microlith (b) and a flake that would be a suitable blank for a neolithic arrowhead (c) (see fig. 9); flakes, seen from the ventral face, produced with a hard hammer (d) and a soft hammer (e) (after Knowles).

3
Manufacture

Beautiful stone implements do not drop out of a struck pebble like a stone from a plum! The finest pieces would have taken many hours of concentrated effort, employing a complex range of tools and methods determined by the raw material selected and the desired end-product. During the period covered here, there was an important change in the variety of tools and methods that an individual would use. This change occurred in Britain at about 4000 BC, coincident with the transition from a hunting-gathering to an agricultural economy. It may be supposed that a new technology was introduced by the colonising farmers from continental Europe. We can begin to understand the changing techniques of stoneworking by comparing some of the tools from either side of this transition. We will start with the arrowhead.

Arrowheads

The essential difference between arrowheads produced in the hunting-gathering era and those in use by the early farmers relates to their method of fabrication. The hunters fashioned their weapons from a *blade*, a long, thin parallel-sided flake with ridges along its entire length, whilst farming period arrowheads were never produced from this basic form (see fig. 9).

All flakes, whatever their characteristics, are struck from *cores*, carefully prepared blocks of stone. Cores must be shaped according to the type of flake essential to the finished implement. Thus the hunter-gatherer prepared his core in a manner specific to blade production, by creating a first ridge (if no such ridge occurred naturally on the nodule selected), producing in the process a triangular-sectioned blade known as a *crested blade* (fig. 10). The characteristic mesolithic flakes with sinuous ridges running the length of a single face could now be struck from a core prepared thus. Ensuing ridges on the core would be narrowly spaced, indicative of a high degree of technical skill. Other flake cores (those generally found in neolithic contexts) demanded less careful preparation, and less control was necessary in flake production. It is much simpler to make a flake for a *bifacial* arrowhead (one with ridges running across both of its faces), the main requirement being an even thickness of appropriate degree. Flakes for this type of implement could easily be made by striking a core at a point between two widely spaced ridges (fig. 11).

Although most flake removal work could have been accomplished with a *hard* stone hammer, experiments have shown that finer results could be achieved with a *soft* hammer rod of antler, wood, bone or horn. Many prehistoric hammer stones – usually conveniently shaped natural pebbles – have been found in Britain, but to date very few soft hammers have been identified, although there is no doubt that soft hammers were widely used in both mesolithic and neolithic eras. Flakes produced by soft or hard hammers can be distinguished, and both types have been discovered in all chronological contexts (see fig. 11). The application of force to the edge of a core *platform*, correctly controlled, will cause a flake to come off the front of the core. On the back, or *ventral* face of the flake, below the point of force, there will be a swelling or *bulb*, with a corresponding hollow in the core. This is one of the characteristic features of conchoidal fracture. In general, a hard hammer will produce a large bulb, and a soft hammer a small or diffuse bulb. A small lip that runs along the ridge between the ventral face and the *butt* (part of the core's platform removed with the flake) and that commonly appears on flakes produced by a soft hammer again betrays the use of this hammer type. It may surprise some readers that stone, particularly flint, can be worked with wood. It is the conchoidal fracture that makes this possible: the break is caused by force waves set up inside the stone, not by the hammer wearing away the stone or cutting through it. An American archaeologist has recalled meeting an elderly ranch owner in Nevada who could remember how, in his childhood, wheel spokes and tool handles were constantly disappearing: the local Indians (stone users) had discovered a convenient source of wooden hammers!

The process of transforming the struck blade or flake (these initial flakes are known as *blanks*) into a usable arrowhead again distinguishes mesolithic and neolithic technology. The hunter first removed the bulb from his blade using the *microburin technique*. The blade was laid on a stone anvil with its ridged, or *dorsal*, face downwards. A notch was worked into the edge with repeated blows from a small hard hammer. At a certain point the blade would snap of its own accord: the characteristic piece of waste is known as a microburin (before their true origin was known through experiment, one interpretation of such pieces was that they were small burins or graving tools). The remaining blade portion needed only a little *retouch* (secondary working) to turn it into a finished point. In Britain this notching technique is only found in mesolithic industries. It is probably the easiest controlled process to carry out in knapping technology (see fig. 12).

The neolithic approach was very different. The edges of the basic

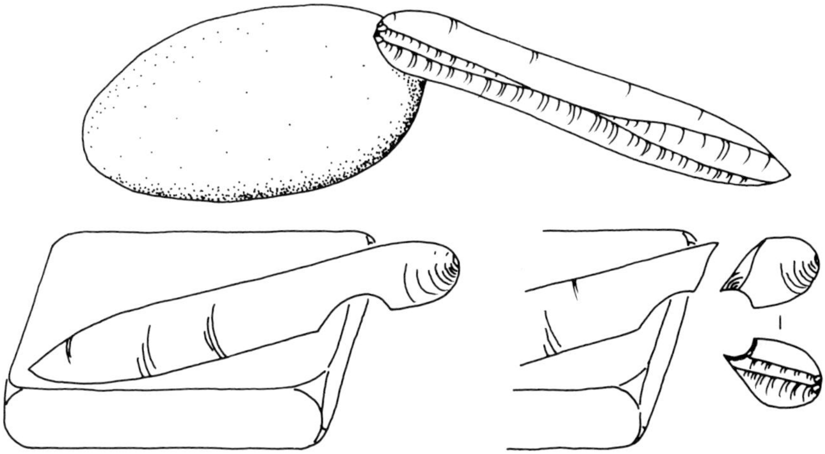

12. Microburin technique. A blade is laid dorsal face down on a stone anvil, and a notch is made with a stone hammer until the blade snaps. The waste piece (lower right) is known as a microburin (after Tixier).

flake were first strengthened by light hammering or crushing designed to create a narrow platform (known as a *turned edge*) from which thinning flakes could be struck. A preform was then created by chipping away the material from each face in turn until little of the original surface remained. The final shaping was done with a pressure-flaker. Small flakes were carefully removed by pressing an antler point against the edge of the preform arrowhead in order to thin the piece and sharpen and straighten the edges. This process often resulted in an impressive pattern of fine, parallel flaking scars. Antler pressure-flakers would have required frequent sharpening, and grooved stones ideal for this purpose have been found in Britain (see fig. 13).

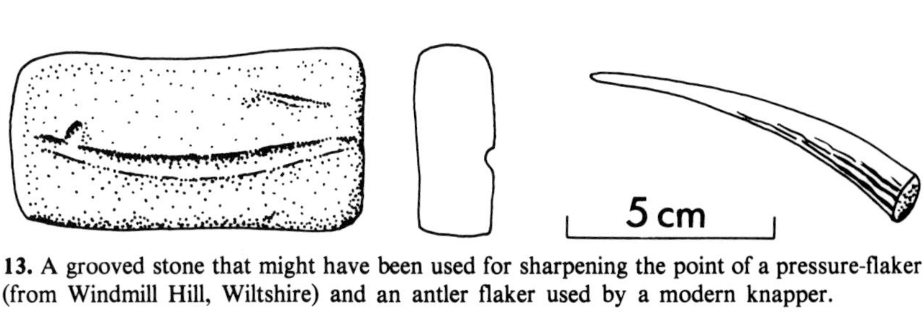

13. A grooved stone that might have been used for sharpening the point of a pressure-flaker (from Windmill Hill, Wiltshire) and an antler flaker used by a modern knapper.

Celts

We shall next consider those implements known as *celts*. This is a useful antiquarian term which encompasses all heavy edge tools including adzes, axes and chisels. The mesolithic adze and the neolithic axe are generally similar in shape but, as with the arrowheads, the production technique is radically different.

A blank for a mesolithic adze was typically a natural nodule of flint carefully selected for its suitable shape (fig. 14). Neolithic man was not so concerned with the form of the nodule as with its ultimate working properties, and some rough flaking was usually necessary to achieve the blank stage (fig. 15). The first distinctive manufacturing features can be seen by looking at the flaked celts in profile (fig. 16 a and b). On the one hand the edge is sinuous, while on the other the edge is straight and slightly faceted. This is because the neolithic celt was given, like the neolithic arrowhead flake, a turned edge. From this edge, flakes would have been removed first down one side, then down the other. The mesolithic adze, however, does not have a turned edge. In this case flakes were removed alternately from each face, each scar serving as a platform for the next removal – a process known as *alternate flaking*.

The creation of the cutting edge constitutes the greatest technological difference between the two periods. This was effected on the mesolithic adze with a deftly delivered single blow from one side. The same method was used to resharpen a worn edge, and the resultant *tranchet flakes* are commonly found. In contrast, the neolithic techniques were laborious and tedious, and yet it is these techniques which have, from the original definition of a 'neolithic age', epitomised not only the stoneworking technology, but the whole 'neolithic achievement': I refer to the techniques of grinding and pecking.

The best material for grinding flint is a quartz-rich sandstone in which the matrix is sufficiently soft to release grains. Severely worn grindstones on which celts were probably shaped have been found in all parts of Britain. The basic work axes of flint were usually ground all over, a process entailing considerable time and effort. Axes made from non-flint rocks were almost invariably completely ground, or, if the stone was more suited to pecking than flaking, pecked all over and ground at the blade edge. Apart from in Ireland, where this technique was practised in the mesolithic, grinding is completely absent in Britain before 4000 BC. How much the innovation was a technical improvement, and to what extent stylistically motivated, has yet to be demonstrated. However, it does seem probable that the smooth outline of a ground celt made it more resistant to shock than its flaked

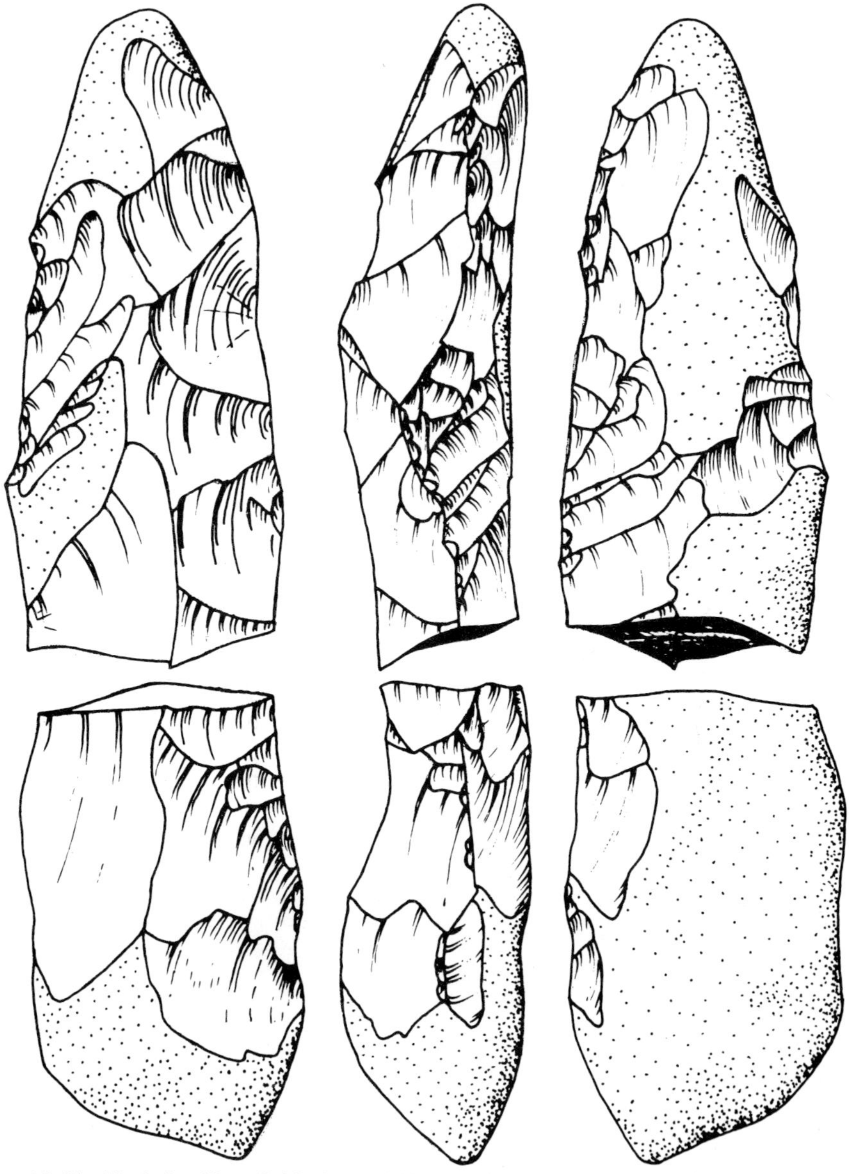

14. The blank for this unfinished mesolithic adze (from Farnham, Surrey) was a sausage-shaped flint nodule. Experimental work has shown that it is quite common for pieces to break in half in this way during manufacture (after Clark).

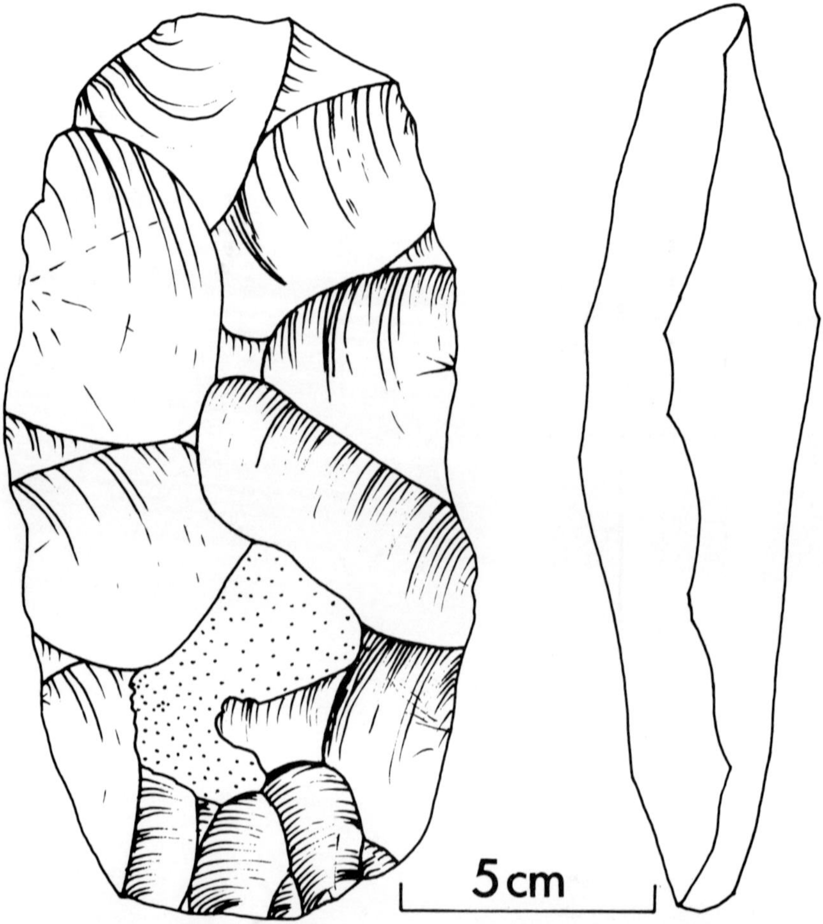

15. A roughly flaked blank for a neolithic axehead (based on an example found in a cache at Lound, Suffolk). Following the usual convention, the cortex (the rough outer crust on flint) is shown dotted.

counterpart – although it probably also made the head harder to fix rigidly into a haft.

Perforated implements

Our final comparison concerns different techniques used to achieve the same end, if not the same tools. Perforated implements (the perforations were probably made for the provision of a handle) are found throughout the period considered here and are almost invariably fashioned from stones without conchoidal fracture – those worked by pecking. Examining the many implements with holes through them, we can see that the perforations are generally of two kinds. Either the

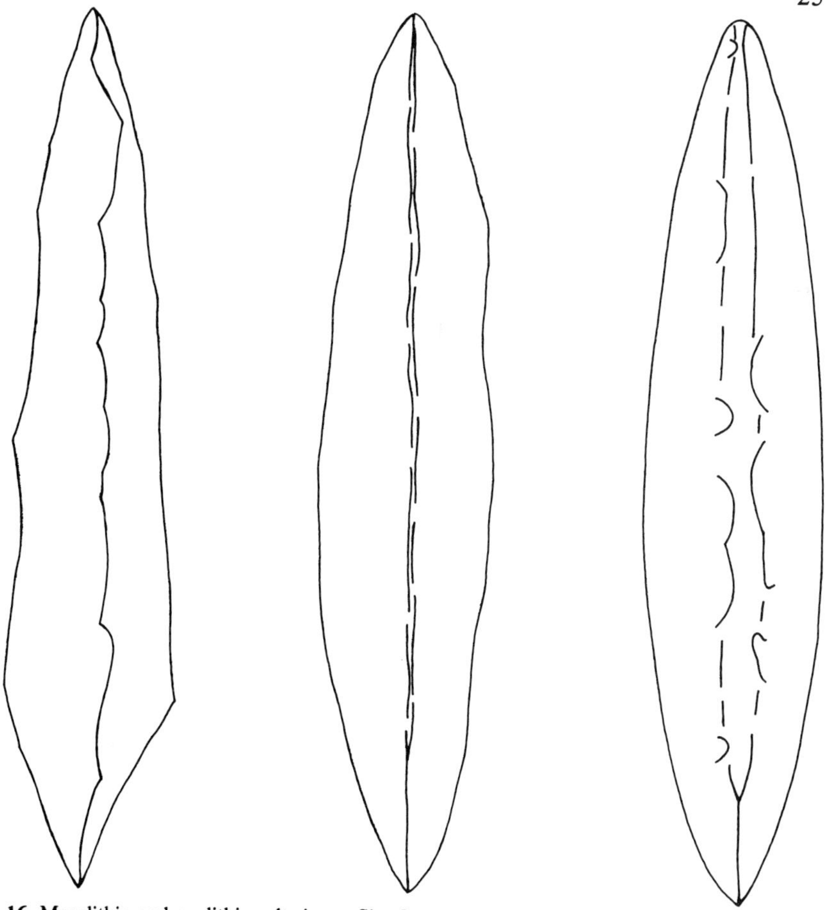

16. Mesolithic and neolithic celts in profile. Contrast the sinuous edge of the mesolithic adze (left) with the straight, slightly faceted edge of the neolithic flaked preform (centre) and the wide facet of the finished ground axe (right).

sides of the hole are straight, or they curve inwards towards the centre, producing an 'hourglass' profile. These different shapes reflect different perforation methods.

The hourglass profile is particularly characteristic of mesolithic technology. Either the prepared implement was pecked from both sides with a hard hammer, the hole being widened by grinding after the central breakthrough was achieved, or the perforation was made with a solid drill, perhaps a wooden rod turned with a bow. In the latter case, friction would cause the drill to wear, thus the hole diameter would decrease towards its centre.

The late neolithic saw the introduction of the hollow drill of wood,

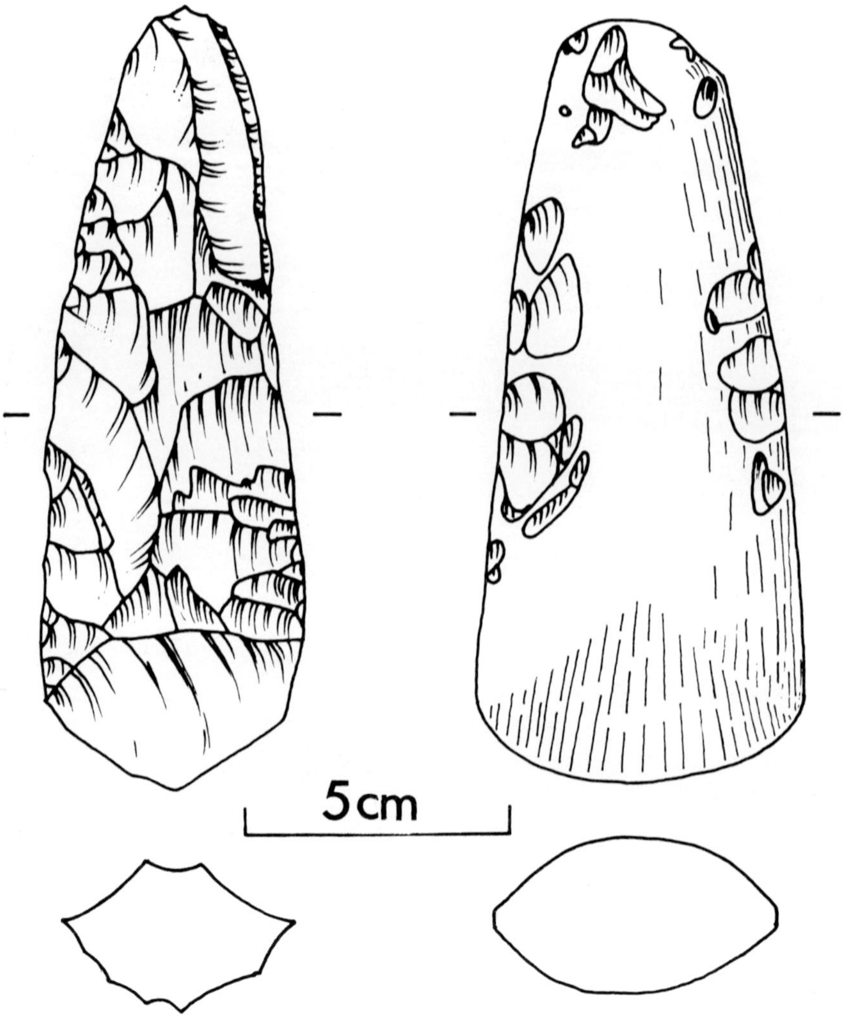

17. A flaked mesolithic adze (left) and a ground neolithic axe (right). The cutting edge of the former was made by removing a flake from the lower end after all the other shaping had been completed. The blow that removed this flake, known as a *tranchet blow*, was delivered on the left side. The stronger, but blunter, edge of the neolithic axe was formed by grinding.

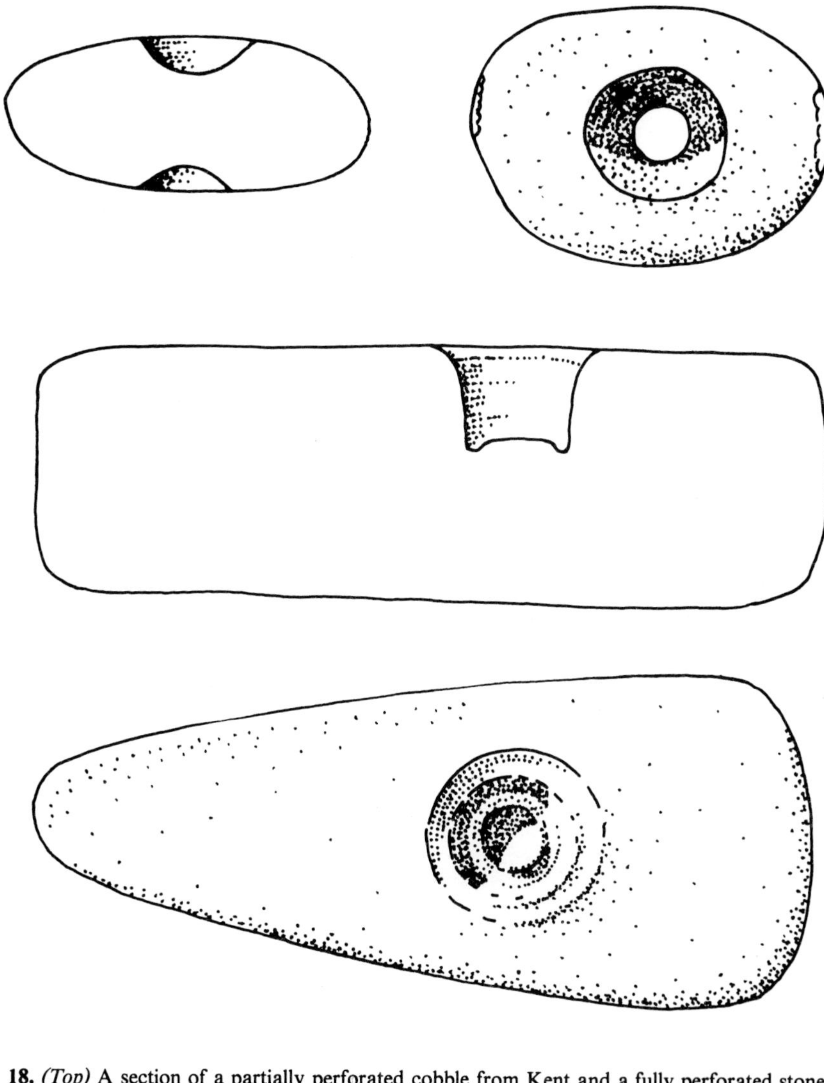

18. *(Top)* A section of a partially perforated cobble from Kent and a fully perforated stone from Hampshire (after Rankine). *(Bottom)* A partially perforated 'axe-hammer' (based on a specimen from Strathclyde). The cobbles are probably mesolithic, the 'hourglass' hole in the Hampshire example being made with a solid drill or by pecking. The vertical-sided hole in the late neolithic axe-hammer was made with a hollow drill.

19. The dished surface on the standing stone in this circle on Penmaenmawr, Gwynedd, was probably made by the grinding of stone axes. The circle is very near an important neolithic stone quarry.

bone or antler (or, when available, copper). With the help of fine sand as an abrasive, this drill type (again bow-turned) cut straight-sided perforations and produced a cylindrical plug of stone as a by-product.

Other lithic techniques

In conclusion, mention must be made of two little discussed lithic techniques, one of which was certainly and the other probably practised during the neolithic. The first is a specialised flaking method known as the Levallois core technique, after the Paris suburb of Levallois-Peret, where some typical finds were made in the nineteenth century. Levallois cores and flakes are commonly present amongst

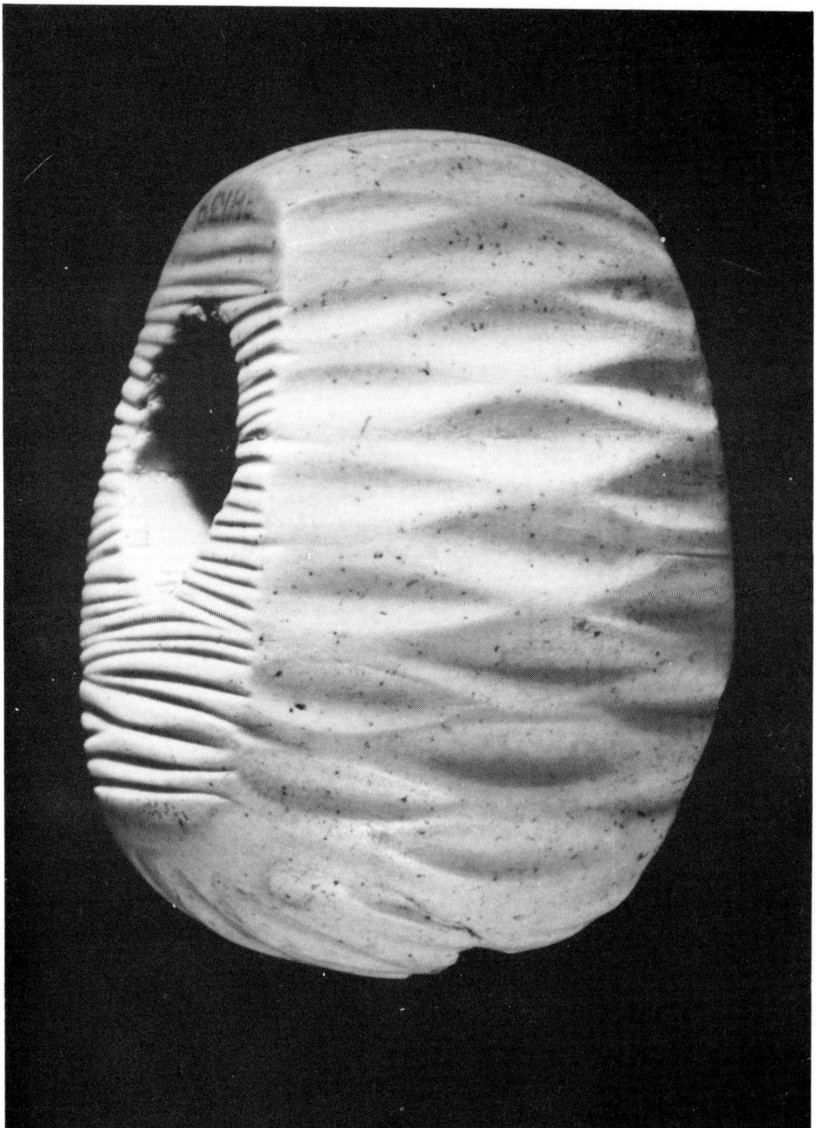

20. A fine 'Maesmore' type 'macehead', an object of unknown function, skilfully made by flaking, grinding and drilling flint. Length 60 millimetres ($2\frac{1}{2}$ inches). (Photograph: National Museum of Antiquities of Scotland.)

flint-mine debris: this association is probably a function of the wasteful nature of the technique, which seems to have been restricted to situations where flint was abundantly available. The process involved the elaborate preparation of a distinctive 'tortoise' core (so called from its typically asymmetric concave shape) from which a single flat, thin, disc-shaped flake would be removed: the core was then probably rejected. It has been suggested that these flakes were intended for conversion into distinctive ground edge tools often called 'knives' (fig. 21). Like so many prehistoric stone tools, however, their precise function is unknown.

The second and final technique to be considered here is the heating of stone before working to improve its flaking qualities. Heating to about 400-550 Centigrade (690-960 Fahrenheit), probably by burial under a fire or hearth, affects the stone in such a way that otherwise poor-quality material becomes workable and good-quality rock can be subjected to finely controlled pressure flaking. It seems that in the neolithic there would have been demands for both of these transformations, although no evidence for the practice has yet been described.

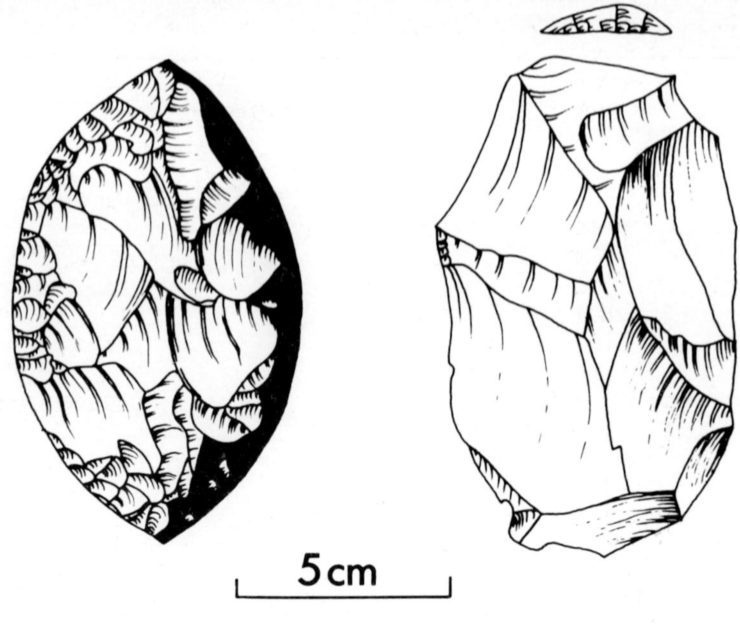

21. *(Right)* A Levallois flake (after Clarke) from a neolithic mine at Grime's Graves, Norfolk. *(Left)* A 'knife' (after Clark) with a ground (shaded) back, from Burnt Fen, Cambridgeshire.

4
Distribution

The considerable distances which separate some neolithic ground stone axes from their geological sources have long been subject to intense speculation. Why did axes move so far, especially when, in some cases, apparently suitable raw materials lay much nearer at hand? This is an intriguing problem, to which there are many possible solutions. It is important to realise, however, that despite the keen interest generated by these markedly scattered distribution patterns work to date has indicated that the great majority of mesolithic and neolithic tools were made from materials local to their area of use. Our first aim therefore will be to examine local distribution mechanisms.

It is likely either that most quarries or outcrops were visited by people wanting stone and quarrying it themselves or that the various sources of raw material were controlled by quarry-owning groups, perhaps local tribes. In the latter case stone would be obtained by direct exchange with the quarry owners.

Fig. 22 shows the known distributions of items from three of the sources that seem to have been exploited in either of these localised ways. A dark, glassy stone – a coarse form of obsidian called pitchstone – that outcrops on the Isle of Arran was used from at least late in the mesolithic, and probably throughout the neolithic, for making small flake tools. All finds of pitchstone implements to date come from Scotland or the extreme north of England. Axes made from a localised outcrop of altered Cornish picrite have been identified by petrologists from spots all over the south-western peninsula, whilst in East Anglia flint axes from a single source, perhaps a quarry, are distributed over an area of similar size. This last source has yet to be identified, but the distinctive nature of both the shape and the material of these axes leaves little doubt as to their common origin. Were we able to characterise flint in very localised terms, it is quite likely that many similar distribution patterns would emerge, some perhaps showing the production of a single tool type, others reflecting the use of a quarry or outcrop for all needs. There is more potential for distribution studies in the highland zone, where a much greater variety of distinctive materials was exploited throughout prehistory.

Although comparatively few in number, the best known quarries are those which produced exceptionally widely distributed ground celts. Four outcrops in particular were especially productive: an extensive tuff series in the Lake District, an augite granophyre in North Wales, some outcrops of porcellanite on the north-east coast of Northern Ireland and a gabbro near Penzance. The usual explanation for the widespread occurrence of axes from these quarries is couched in terms of modern trading. Entrepreneurs started a quarry and sought out distant markets by extensive voyaging: indeed, the quarries are often referred to as 'axe factories'. But of all the possible explanations, this is by far the least plausible. It is much more likely that these extended distributions developed in much the same manner as the localised patterns just discussed.

Fig. 23 shows the distribution of *caches*, small groups of tool blanks or preforms that were buried and never recovered (caches of finished tools are also found, but we are not concerned with these here). Most of these are close to their probable sources, rarely occurring outside a fairly localised zone. Direct contact with the source area would thus seem to be fairly short range, suggesting that local inhabitants either obtained preforms or blanks through exchange with the quarry owners or themselves procured the raw material which was freely accessible.

It would seem, in most cases, that the only difference between the small and the large quarries lies in the number of objects produced. When the quantity of products was high, there would inevitably be more axes in circulation in the near vicinity at any one time and hence more opportunities for people at a greater distance to obtain the axes by exchange. In such a fashion, axes could travel slowly about from hand to hand, eventually being lost or broken many miles from their source. There need be no defined 'trade routes', for the exchanges could take place at chance or prearranged meetings between individuals; and such meetings need not have been in a market – indeed they almost certainly were not so.

We can probably explain in the same manner the presence in Britain of celts from the European mainland (fig. 25). The four stone axes of dolerite from Brittany are outliers of a very dense distribution in north-western France and are identifiable by their distinctive mineralogical composition. The Scandinavian flint celts (and also a few flint daggers), however, are distinguishable only by their shape, principally by their characteristic squarish section. It is quite possible that other axes from the Continent have been found in Britain but lie unrecognised because of their similar shape to insular flint celts. It is likely that at least some of the jade axes reached Britain from Europe as items of value rather than of day-to-day use. It is clear from both the rarity of the material and their exceptionally fine workmanship that many of these implements were never intended for anything other

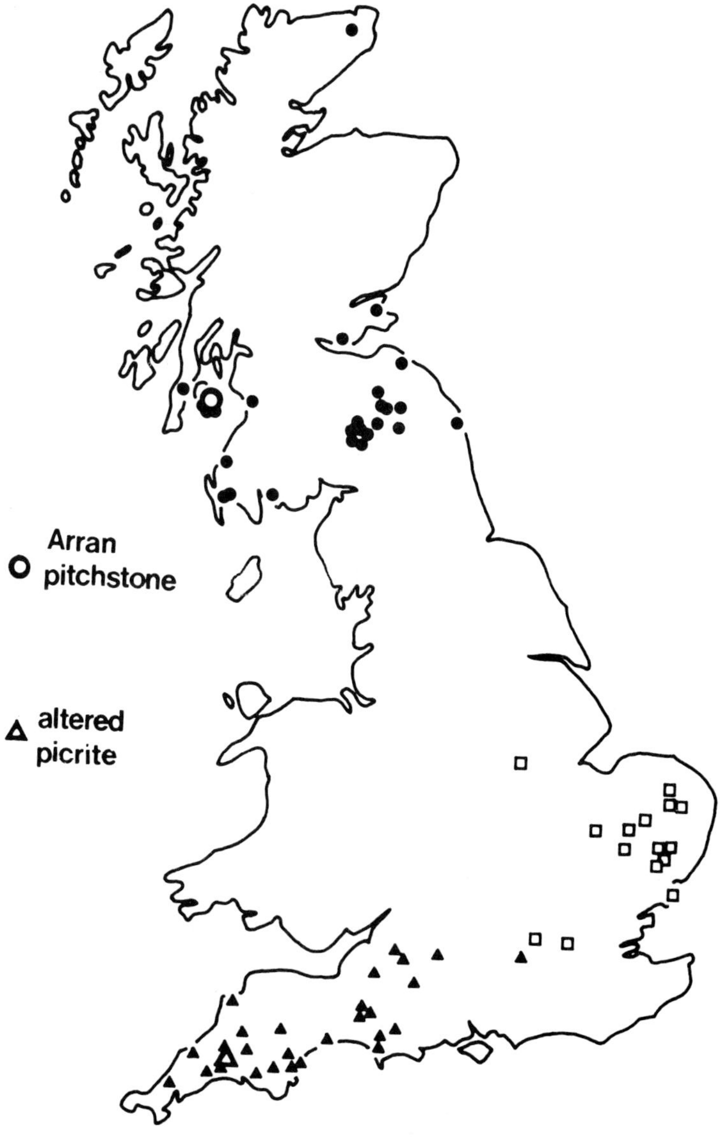

22. The known distribution of flake tools of Arran pitchstone, axes of altered picrite from near Callington, Cornwall, and eastern flint axes with no precisely determined source. All these products remained relatively close to their places of origin.

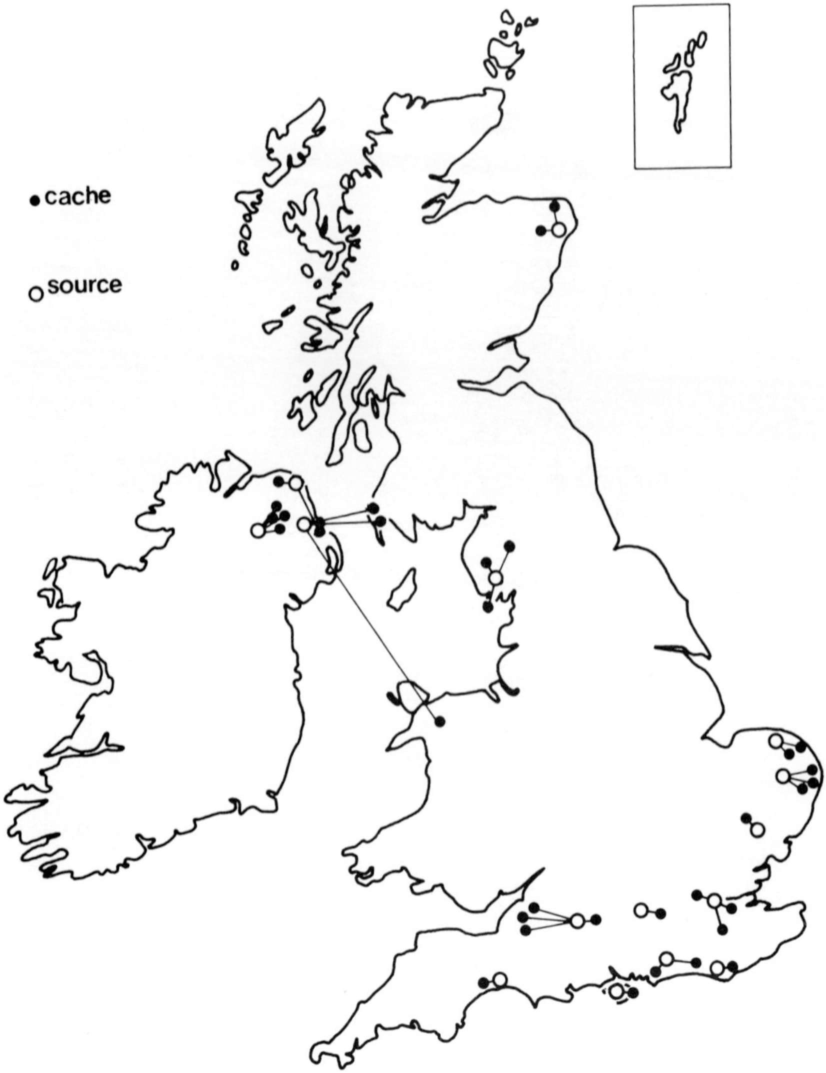

23. Caches of flint flakes or unfinished stone celts connected to the nearest likely source.

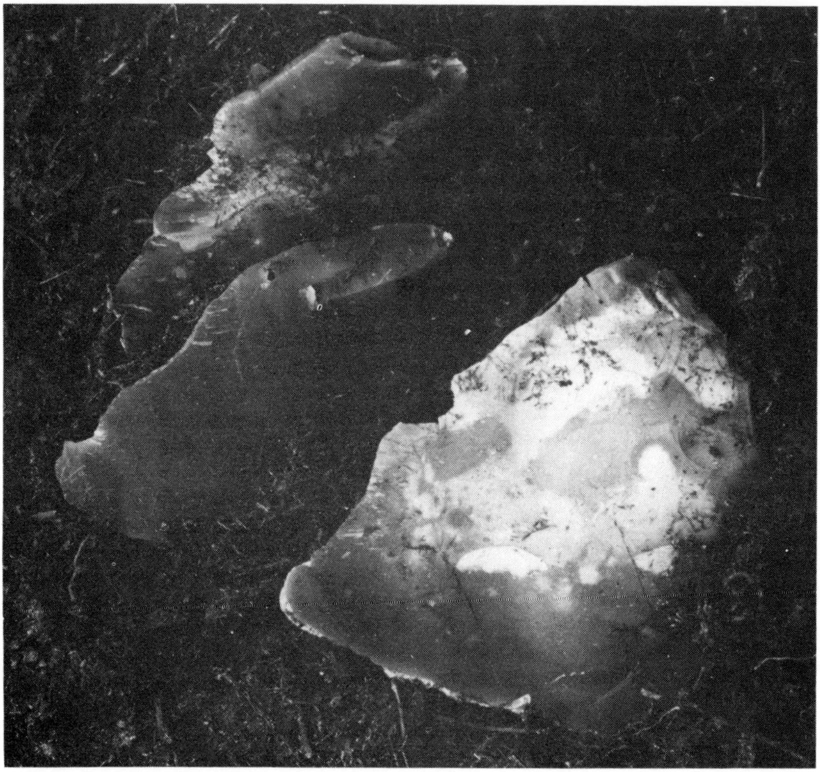

24. In about 2000 BC someone lost twelve flint flakes wrapped in moss and cotton-grass in the marshes of the Somerset Levels. They were found during peat cutting in 1977. Three of the flakes can be seen in this photograph protruding from the moss. (Photograph: Somerset Levels Project.)

than treasuring and displaying. Nonetheless, their wide distribution could still be a product of a 'down-the-line' exchange system, the fine objects passing from one individual to another and staying in circulation over several generations.

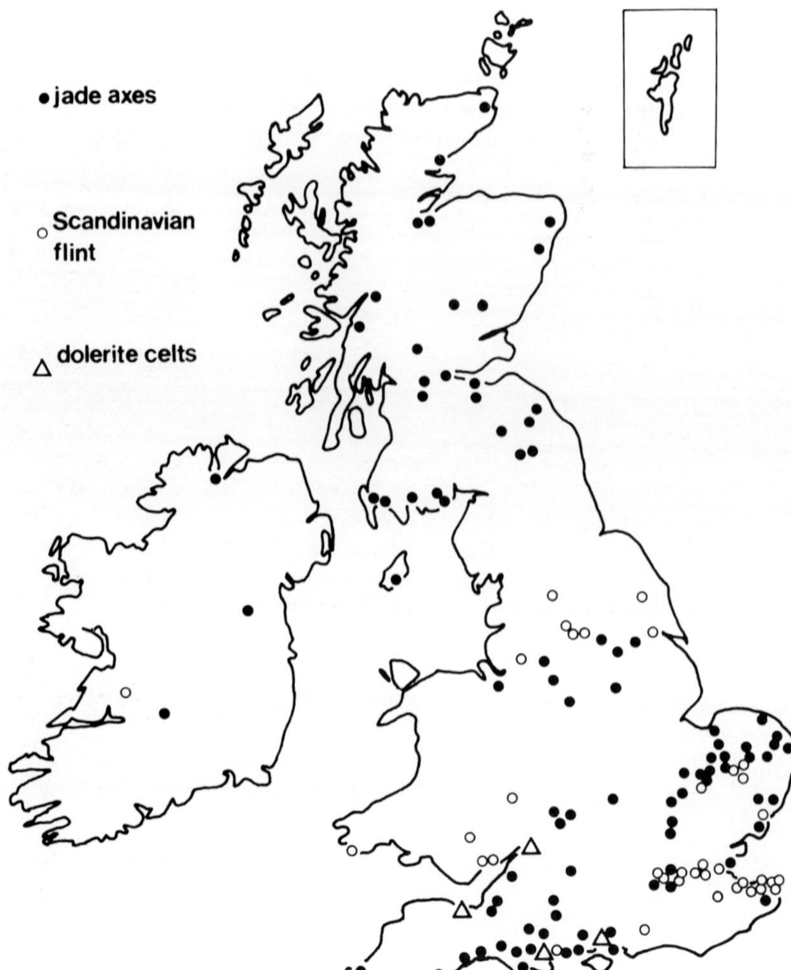

25. Distribution of stone implements made on the European continent: jade axes, Scandinavian flint celts and daggers, and dolerite celts from Brittany.

5
Use

The explorations of the sixteenth and seventeenth centuries gradually revealed to Europe new worlds peopled by societies with totally alien cultures and technologies. The more observant travellers and intellectuals began to see similarities between some of the items in use in the Americas and mysterious objects found in the ground in Europe. The Italian physician Mercati was quick to recognise that stone objects generally held to be the magical creations of forces in thunderstorms were, in reality, man-made. In 1686 Dr Robert Plot was able to do the same for stone celts found in Britain, informing a slightly incredulous readership that 'how they might be fastened to a helve may be seen in the Museum Ashmoleanum, where there are several Indian ones of the like kind fitted up in the same order as when formerly used'. The other general category of tool that came to be recognised by analogy with implements in use by 'primitive' peoples was the 'scraper', a flake with strengthening retouch on its edges.

Comparison of prehistoric implements with those in use by recent stone-using peoples in other parts of the world is one way of inferring a function for the objects that fill our museums. It is a small step from this to using the general shapes of implements as pointers in the same direction. One piece, for example, may fit snugly in the hand in such a way that a sharp cutting edge is exposed, whilst the narrow point of another appears eminently suited to the piercing of leather. This seemingly obvious way to interpret stone tools can, however, be very misleading. If we look closely at our ethnographic people, we can observe them using the same objects in different ways. In one such case in aboriginal Australia, a finely flaked biface might be first used as a spearhead, then, by the tribe that received it through exchange, as a fighting knife, before finally ending its days as a treasured curio of unknown function! It is quite common to find axes and adzes of identical shape, and in one area a special handle was devised that enabled the blade to be turned around so that it could function in both ways alternately. It is well to bear this sort of instance in mind when we talk about neolithic 'axes'.

An additional problem arises from a heavy reliance on shape as a guide to function. Characteristics resulting from the manufacturing process of a particular implement are often misinterpreted as indicators of the way the implement was used. Furthermore, waste flakes and fragments (called *debitage*) have been mistakenly described as intentionally produced tools. We have already seen how the by-product of the microburin technique was thought to be a tool, incredible though this now seems for such a small fragment. Serious mistakes have also been made in the interpretation of curiously shaped natural stones as functional pieces!

Whilst the shapes of worked stones may *suggest* a function, this suggestion must be reinforced by other lines of evidence. One of the most important of these is *use wear study*. Use wear studies essentially began in the nineteenth century, when Sir John Evans examined the effect of scraping surfaces such as wood or bone with a flint tool. He found that the scraping action resulted in the removal of small flakes or chips from the working edge of the tool. In the 1930s the Sussex archaeologist Cecil Curwen experimented with flint blades and flakes to confirm that certain glosses and polishes observable on the edge of some neolithic flakes were produced during use, specifically by friction between the flint and straw or wood. The most obvious of these effects is known as *sickle gloss* and indicates that a piece has been used for cutting straw, grass or reeds. Sickle gloss is common on neolithic flakes but has never been found on mesolithic implements.

Recently archaeologists have been looking at the effects of implement use in detail and have discovered that not only are there a great many different types of wear but that, through experimenting with 'modern' stone tools, it is often possible to suggest how the wear was caused. Microscopic examination is required throughout use wear studies, but the scarring observed by Evans and the polish described by Curwen demand different techniques: low magnification (forty to sixty times) and high magnification (two hundred times, or up to ten thousand times with a scanning electron microscope) respectively. The most productive work so far has been achieved with high magnifications. In ideal conditions, it has been found possible not only to identify the part of the tool used and the way it was held but even the type of material worked – meat, plant fibre, wood and so on. However, ideal conditions are relatively rare in Britain. Patination, for example, which affects most flintwork from southern England, completely obscures any fine polish or abrasion. Despite such problems, careful search frequently reveals material suitable for microscopic analysis, and work is in progress at several centres throughout Britain. Already the results of work both in Britain and elsewhere have discredited the popular assumptions that all tools were retouched and that shaped edges were necessarily working edges. 'Microwear' studies have thus made it possible to identify as tools pieces that to the naked eye look like nothing more than waste flakes.

A second possible line of evidence to test functional inference concerns the objects found in association with the piece in question.

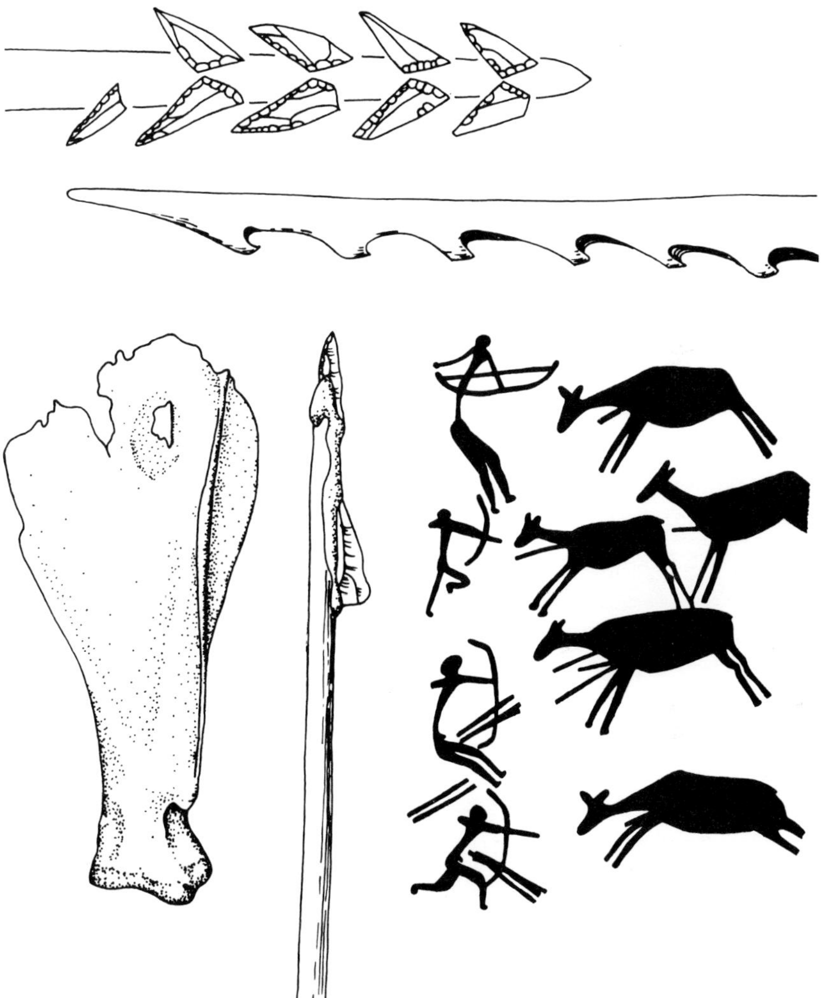

26. Hunting with stone tools in the mesolithic. The pine arrow, tipped with microliths mounted in resin, was excavated in Scania. No such finds have been made in Britain, but the microliths (top) from the Pennines were discovered lying in this arrangement, suggesting a spearhead. Below is a flint-carved antler harpoon barb from Star Carr, North Yorkshire. Also from Star Carr is the elk scapula (lower left): the hole was made by a flint-tipped missile, which failed to kill the animal, for the wound had healed. On the right is part of a rock painting in Spain depicting the hunting of red deer (after Clark, Jacobi and Noe-Nygaard).

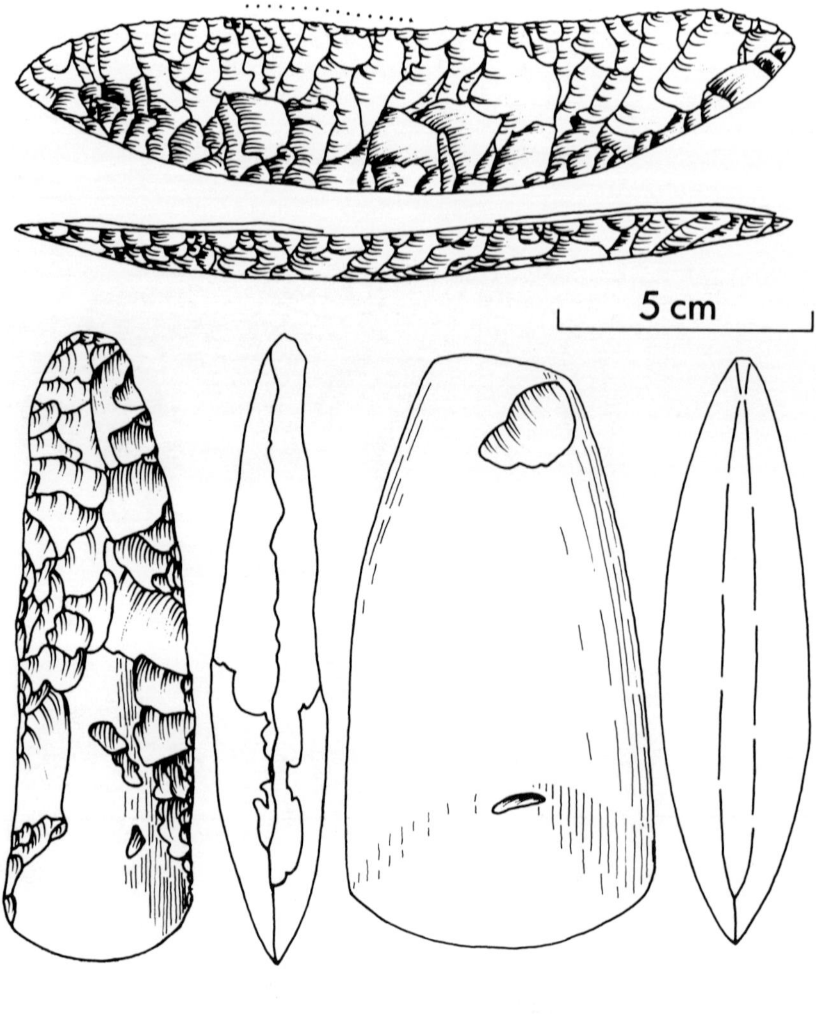

27. A cache of flint tools from East Knoyle, Wiltshire, suggesting a farmer's field kit: a reaping knife (top), a partly ground adze (left) and a fully ground axe (right). The dots along the cutting edge of the knife show where 'sickle gloss' developed (after Smallcombe).

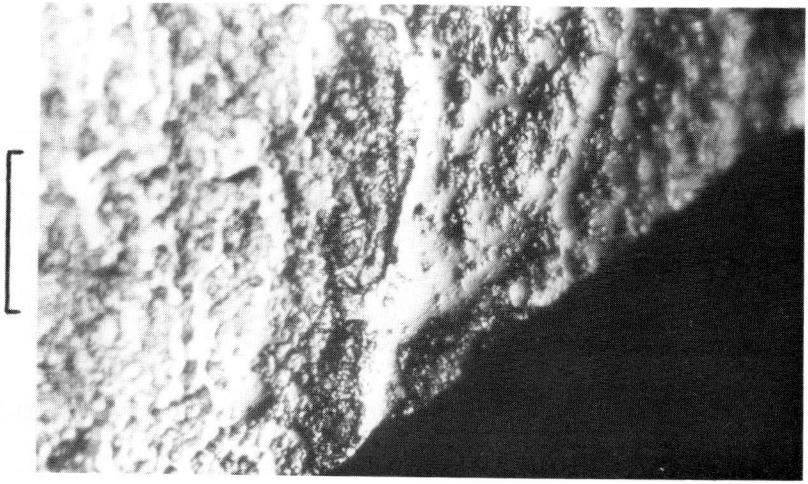

28. Two photographs of wear on a flint surface caused by reaping wheat, taken at a magnification of 140 times (top) and 280 times (bottom) by Emily Moss. This most striking form of use wear, commonly known as 'sickle gloss', is caused by the silica in plant stems. The wear was experimentally produced by Phil Harding, who also made the reaping knife. Scales 0.1 mm.

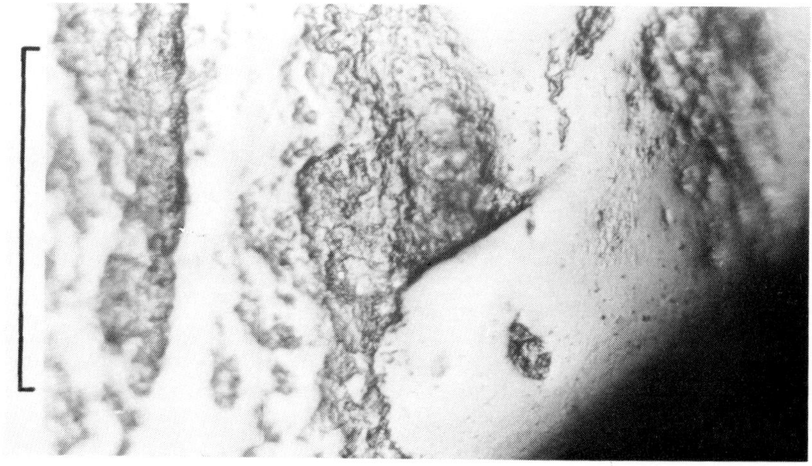

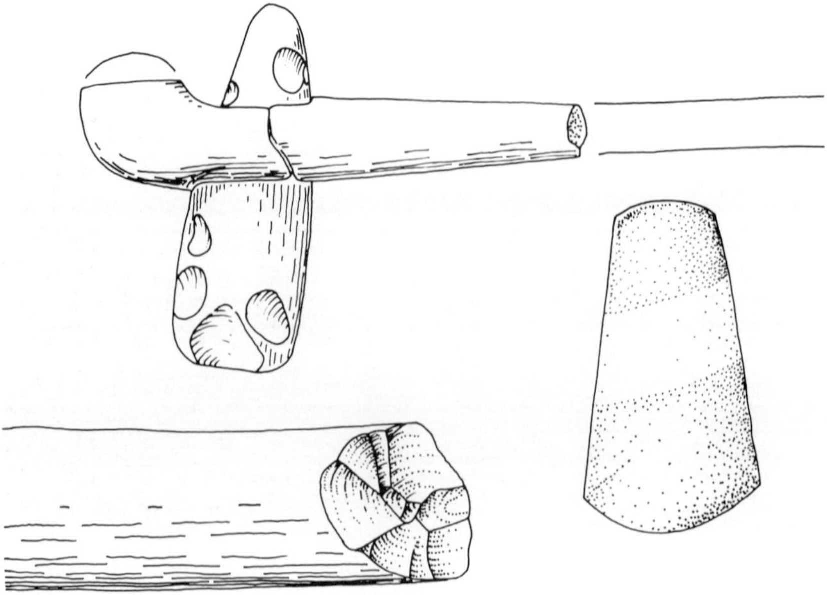

29. *(Top)* A neolithic axe blade of green tuff, in its original wooden handle, from Cumbria. *(Bottom right)* An axe blade stained by peat, with an unstained band where the stone was covered by a handle. *(Bottom left)* The chopped end of a wooden peg from the Somerset Levels (after Coles).

Conditions favourable to preservation often provide informative associated material. For example, a number of stone celts (all axes) in their original wooden handles were found during nineteenth-century agricultural improvements. All had survived in peat, an ideal medium for the preservation of organic material. In addition to preserving the wood, the peat had stained the stone, leaving a clear band where the celt was protected by its handle. Many neolithic celts with similar bands across them have been unearthed and we can infer that these too were hafted as axes, although no handles were recovered. All the celts thus far identified as axeheads are very similar in shape. It is therefore logical to suggest that celts of very different shape also differed in function. Examination of wear on the blade edges and the efficiency of experimental copies in various task roles (as adzes or chisels for example) would help to test this theory.

Another promising association concerns mortuary practice. Individuals were often buried with their personal possessions, or perhaps special offerings. Although such burials occur but rarely

30. Neolithic archery. *(Top left)* Two grooved stones thought to be for straightening arrow shafts; from a burial in Hertfordshire. *(Bottom right)* A slightly curved stone wristguard (this example had gold-studded pins for attachment). Both of these objects are typical items commonly found associated with male burials. *(Right)* This arrow was found in a bog in Grampian in the nineteenth century. *(Centre)* This man is drawing a modern replica of a remarkable neolithic bow found in the Somerset Levels (after Clark).

prior to the late neolithic, they invariably yield useful information. It is quite common, for example, to find one or two flint flakes in a grave, suggesting that unretouched flakes *were* used: a clear case for microwear analysis. Iron pyrites is commonly found in burials together with pieces of flint, suggesting a fire-making kit. This material, found in other contexts without its associated flint strikers would be difficult to interpret. Archery equipment frequently occurs, always associated with male skeletons. Sometimes a man was buried with just one arrow (and presumably also his bow), but occasionally whole quivers were placed in the grave, containing, in one instance, as many as thirteen arrows. Rarely, arrowheads are found in more gruesome positions. A skeleton recently excavated at Stonehenge had the tips of two projectile points embedded in his chest and may even have been shot from both front and rear simultaneously.

The purpose of this section has been to demonstrate that it is rarely possible to pick up a stone tool from its display case and pronounce on its function. The use of a tool can only be understood through careful consideration of all those forms of evidence discussed above. Manufacturing technology (identified both through observation and through experimental work), use wear study (again involving experiments with imitation tools, as well as examination of the ancient specimens) and associations are all equally important to an appreciation of implement function.

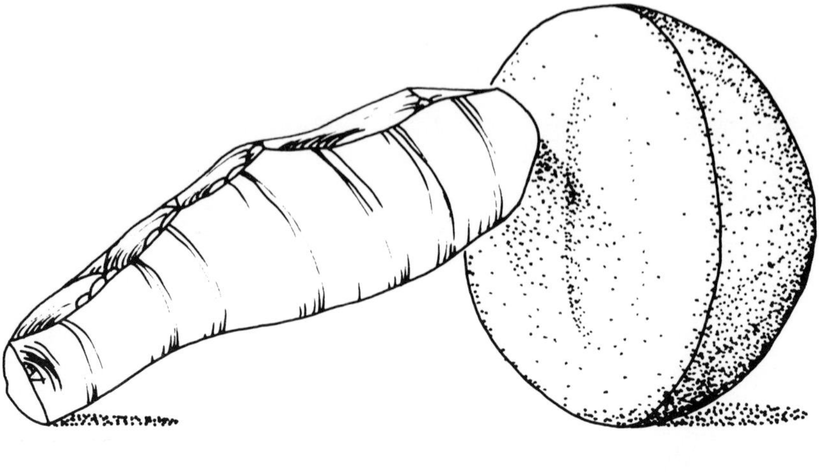

31. A neolithic fire-making kit: an artificially shaped nodule of iron pyrites and a flint striker found together in a grave near Rudstone, Humberside, in 1870 (after Evans).

6
Change

We have already seen how the types of stone tools being made in prehistoric Britain changed dramatically when farmers brought new technologies with them from the European mainland. However, this sudden replacement of one tradition with another was only one change, albeit the most sudden and easily recognisable to the archaeologist, in a complex of traditions of technology and style that was continuously alive and sensitive to change in all aspects of the stone-using societies. How do we measure this change?

Unfortunately, there is no easy answer to this question. The usual method used by archaeologists to date artefacts depends on these artefacts being found in undisturbed stratigraphic contexts. Everything in a single context can thus be assumed to have been in use at the same time. With luck, the finds will include some organic material such as charcoal or antler that will enable a radiocarbon determination to be made, and the estimate of date that this provides can be applied to all objects in the deposit. The current scarcity of undisturbed contexts from the period we are considering is a problem, but there seems no reason why excavation should not slowly fill this gap. However, the greatest impediment to precise chronological determinations arises from the indestructible nature of stone tools and debitage. If we walk over a newly ploughed field virtually anywhere in southern England, we are certain before long to find some prehistoric stone tools. If we were to dig a hole in this field and bury a tin can, some six thousand year old flint flakes might find their way into the pit as we backfilled it. In precisely the same way, a prehistoric ditch may contain stone tools and waste that were already thousands of years old when the ditch was dug. In other words, all of the stone objects in a deposit need not be contemporary. In practice, it is not usually very difficult to recognise this sort of situation, for if all the pieces *are* contemporary and derive from stoneworking activity nearby, then they will be in fresh condition, and it should be possible to fit together some of the flakes. Clearly we must not consider individual tools in isolation, but rather we should look at complete *assemblages* (well contexted groups of finds). It is only by looking at tools and waste products, both of which were equally susceptible to change, that we can begin to understand how the tools themselves were made and used.

A further problem, relating this time only to implements and not to

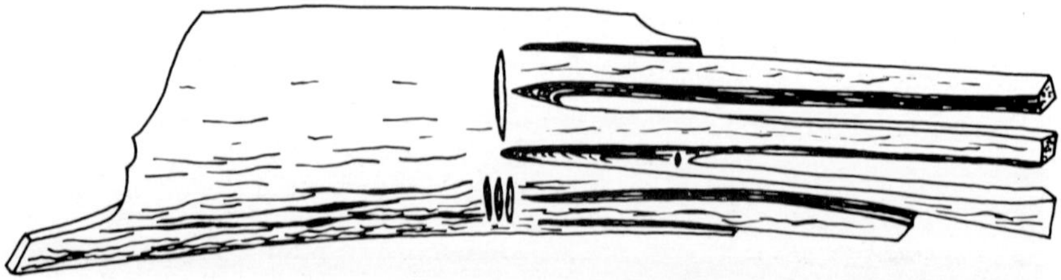

32. A piece of antler shaped by a flint tool; from Windmill Hill, Wiltshire. This neolithic artefact is either a blank for an antler 'comb' or a waste product from antler pin manufacture (after Smith).

their by-products, concerns again the durability of stone. It would have been possible for items to have been handed down from one generation to the next over a considerable period. One would expect particularly fine pieces to have been the most likely candidates for such treatment, called by archaeologists *curation*. It thus follows that a fine flint 'dagger' found in a grave could have two 'dates': one when it was made, and another when it was buried. Both of these events are obviously of great interest, but separating them requires very careful thought.

There is an absolute dating technique that may be able to help us, although in Britain it has not yet been applied to lithic studies. The minerals in any stone become irradiated by natural radio-isotopes. Quartz, the major constituent of flint, traps electrons released by this process but loses them all if it is heated above 380 Centigrade (650 Fahrenheit), when continuing irradiation will start rebuilding the quantity of trapped electrons. It is possible to say when the heating occurred by measuring the effects of this post-heating irradiation with the technique of *thermoluminescence*. Possibilities for using this method exist not only for pieces accidentally dropped into a fire or cremated in a death ceremony, but also for stone that was deliberately heated before it was worked. The potential of this untried approach is massive.

Despite all of these problems, however, it has been possible for archaeologists to make a number of general observations about the way stone industries changed over the eight thousand years or so covered by this book. Several gradual changes take place over the entire period, apparently independent of the mesolithic-neolithic transition. The first of these is a steady decline in the number of fine thin blades produced. Early mesolithic industries were based on the shaping of blade cores, but by the time bronze technology was introduced in Britain true blades were nowhere being made. As basic flake forms

33. When this neolithic skeleton was excavated, a flint arrowhead of the type illustrated in fig. 34 (d) was found in its ribs. The point may well have been responsible for the individual's death in about 3000 BC. (Photograph: Fengate Excavations.)

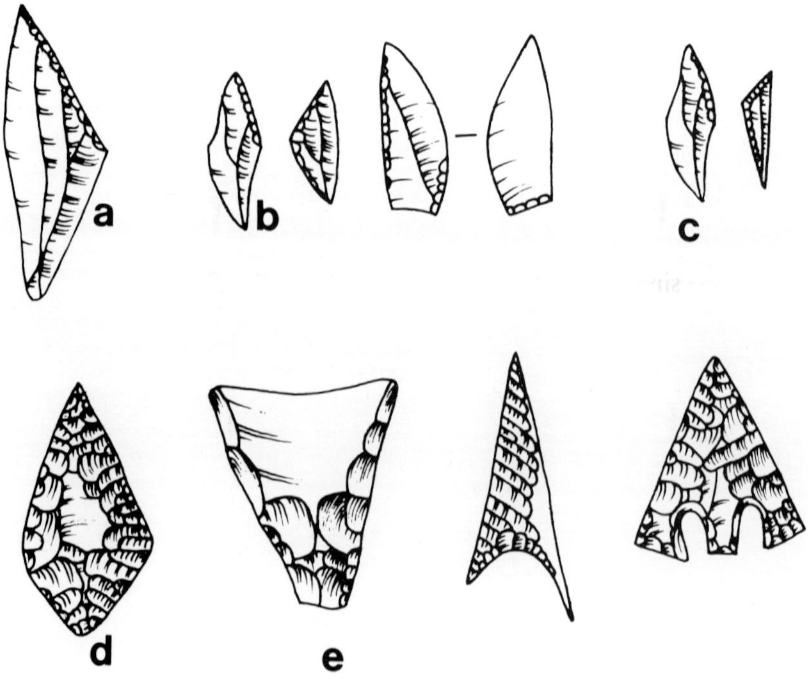

34. Common types of flint projectile points and barbs of various dates: early mesolithic (a), later mesolithic (b and c), early neolithic (d) and late neolithic (e).

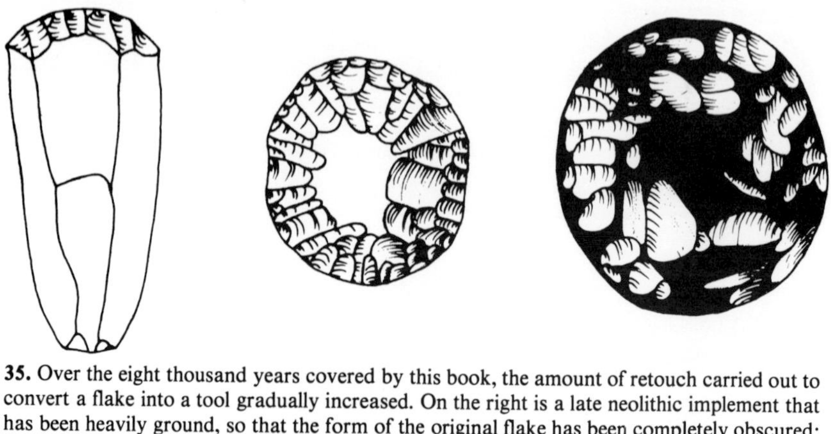

35. Over the eight thousand years covered by this book, the amount of retouch carried out to convert a flake into a tool gradually increased. On the right is a late neolithic implement that has been heavily ground, so that the form of the original flake has been completely obscured; the mesolithic scraper on the left is little different from the untouched flake from which it was made.

changed, so did finishing techniques. Over the centuries more and more time was spent on shaping a flake, both by fine retouch and by grinding. These basically technological developments had stylistic repercussions, and perhaps causes. The chronology of changes in tool styles is only vaguely understood, although fairly clear patterns are beginning to emerge in the field of projectile barbs and heads. However, the relative dating of changes in these implements during the later neolithic has still to be resolved (figs. 34 and 35).

Changes in lithic industries took place within a changing society. Just as no single factor was responsible for social change, so no single factor governed changes in the manufacture and use of stone tools. Change in the availability of raw materials, allied to changing control of raw material resources, may be considered as one possible explanation for some lithic developments; a change in craft practices or methods of food production, each requiring different tool kits, another. The appearance of skilfully made 'daggers' might relate to social status and the inception of a social hierarchy. Property consciousness and the length of time an individual expected to keep an implement (or 'curate' it) could affect the amount of effort expended on its manufacture. The range of possibilities is as wide as human society is complex.

7
What can you do?

Social and economic changes since the nineteenth century have led to the gradual demise of the 'library collector' with an army of farmworkers and labourers eager to augment their meagre wage by scanning the ground for saleable prehistoric stones. Large collections acquired in this way eventually found their way into many of our museums. Most of them, however, are archaeologically worthless, consisting of implements with only the vaguest of provenances. The academic value of an artefact is never intrinsic but rather depends on the quality of the information which surrounds it. It is for this reason that, despite several generations of fieldwork that have produced little of substantial worth, earlier British prehistory is quite capable of being revolutionised as a result of properly thought out fieldwalking programmes. This is where concerned and enthusiastic members of the public can be of inestimable assistance to the archaeologist. The key to success in field collection lies in careful planning and, above all, in asking the right questions. The chances of there being an existing project near you are growing: if there is, take advantage of it. Fieldwalking is a skill, much like excavation technique, that is best acquired by informed experience. Occasional courses (dealing with surface collecting) are run by adult education centres, and there is a slowly growing literature on the subject that should be consulted.

The most important advice I would offer, whatever the field of interest or research, is to gain some experience of knapping. If you are lucky, you will be able to attend a day or weekend course. If not, study the published material on stoneworking technology, then obtain some stone (preferably flint) and simply hammer it to pieces. A few minutes of such activity is worth hours of work in a library, and the 'feel' you should ultimately acquire is invaluable, if it only teaches you that intuitive judgements about lithic technology are usually wrong! One word of warning: when you start knapping flint, you are advised to wear a pair of old leather gloves. The prehistoric popularity of flint was partly based on its sharpness.

The *Lithic Studies Society* has as its object 'the advancement of knowledge of, and education and research in, lithic studies' and organises regular meetings in Britain. For further information, write to The Secretary, Lithic Studies Society, c/o National Museum of Wales, Cardiff, CF1 3NP.

Glossary

Many terms are defined in the text: see index.

Artefact: a product of human action. Defined thus, stone artefacts include tools, debitage and otherwise untouched stones removed from their natural context.

Assemblage: all the artefacts from an undisturbed archaeological context. The distinction between the complete assemblage and the assemblage actually recovered by excavation (which, unless very fine sieves are used, will certainly be incomplete) should always be kept in mind.

Collection: stone artefacts recovered by archaeologists are very frequently not found in close association. The commonest source of such material is the ploughed field surface. In such instances, there is no reason for assuming that any of the pieces are contemporary, and the group is referred to as a collection. The types of analysis that can successfully be applied to collections and assemblages are clearly different.

Industry: a number of contemporary assemblages are frequently found to contain more or less the same range of implement forms and debitage. If these assemblages occur in a contiguous area, they are referred to collectively as an industry (in Britain, the word 'tradition' is used in the same sense).

Mesolithic: the period between about 10,000 and 4000 BC when people lived by hunting and gathering wild foods.

Neolithic: the period between about 4000 and 2000 BC when people subsisted on an agricultural economy.

Bibliography

This select list contains many references which themselves have excellent bibliographies.

Raw materials

Clough, T. H. McK. and W. A. Cummins (eds), 1979. Stone axe studies. *Council for British Archaeology Research Report* no. 23.

Coles, J. M., 1971. The early settlement of Scotland: excavations at Morton, Fife. *Proceedings of the Prehistoric Society* 37.2, 284-366.

Curwen, E. C., 1954. *The Archaeology of Sussex*. London. (For the South Downs flint mines, including Cissbury.)

Jope, E. M., 1952. Porcellanite axes from factories in north-east Ireland: Tievebulliagh and Rathlin. *Ulster Journal of Archaeology* 15, 31-55.

Sieveking, G. de G., *et al*, 1973. A new survey of Grime's Graves – first report. *Proceedings of the Prehistoric Society* 39, 182-218.

Stone, J. F. S., 1935. Excavations at Easton Down, Winterslow, 1933-4. *Wiltshire Archaeological and Natural History Magazine* 47, 68-80.

Manufacture

Crabtree, D. E., 1972. An introduction to flintworking. *Occasional Papers of the Idaho State University Museum,* no. 28.

Johnson, L. L., 1978. A history of flint-knapping experimentation 1838-1976. *Current Anthropology* 19.2, 337-72.

Knowles, H. S., 1953 (reprinted 1976). Stone-worker's progress. *Occasional Papers on Technology* (Pitt Rivers Museum, Oxford), no. 6.

Rowlett, R. M., *et al*, 1974. The interpretation and dating of humanly worked siliceous materials by thermoluminescent analysis. *Proceedings of the Prehistoric Society* 40, 37-44.

Tixier, J. (translated from the French by M. Newcomer), 1974. Glossary for the description of stone tools. *Newsletter of Lithic Technology: Special Publication* no. 1.

Distribution

Clark, J. G. D., 1965. Traffic in stone axe and adze blades. *Economic History Review* 18, 1-28.

Elliott, K., D. Ellman and I. Hodder, 1978. The simulation of neolithic axe dispersal in Britain. In I. Hodder (ed), *Simulation Studies in Archaeology* (Cambridge University Press), 79-81.

Use

Cahen, D., L. H. Keeley and F. L. Van Noten, 1979. Stone tools, toolkits, and human behaviour in prehistory. *Current Anthropology* 20.4, 661-83. (A remarkable illustration of the potential of well contexted assemblages; by fitting together flakes from various parts of a camp floor, the authors were able to throw much light on the activities of its prehistoric occupants.)

Coles, J., 1973. *Archaeology by Experiment.* London.

Curwen, E. C., 1930. Prehistoric flint sickles. *Antiquity* 4, 179-86.

Keeley, L. H. and M. H. Newcomer, 1977. Microwear analysis of experimental flint tools: a test case. *Journal of Archaeological Science* 4, 29-62.

Change

Jacobi, R. M., 1976. Britain inside and outside mesolithic Europe. *Proceedings of the Prehistoric Society* 42, 67-84.

Pitts, M. W. and R. M. Jacobi, 1979. Some aspects of change in flaked stone industries of the mesolithic and neolithic in southern Britain. *Journal of Archaeological Science* 6, 163-77.

Descriptions of some good representative assemblages

Clark, J. G. D., 1954. *Excavations at Star Carr.* Cambridge. (Early mesolithic.)

Clark, J. G. D. and W. F. Rankine, 1939. Excavations at Farnham, Surrey (1937-8): the Horsham Culture and the question of mesolithic dwellings. *Proceedings of the Prehistoric Society* 5.1, 61-118. (Later mesolithic.)

O'Malley, M. and R. M. Jacobi, 1978. The excavation of a mesolithic occupation site at Broom Hill, Braishfield, Hampshire. *Rescue Archaeology in Hampshire* 4, 16-38. (Later mesolithic.)

Smith, I. F., 1965. *Windmill Hill and Avebury.* Oxford. (Early and late neolithic.)

Wainwright, G. J. and I. H. Longworth, 1971. *Durrington Walls: Excavations 1966-1968.* London. (Late neolithic.)

Woodman, P. C., 1977. Recent excavations at Newferry, Co. Antrim. *Proceedings of the Prehistoric Society* 43, 155-99. (Irish mesolithic.)

Studies of particular implement types

Clark, J. G. D., 1928. Discoidal polished flint knives – their typology and distribution. *Proceedings of the Prehistoric Society of East Anglia* 6, 41-54.

Clark, J. G. D., 1932. Note on some flint daggers of Scandinavian type from the British Isles. *Man* 32, 186-90.

Clark, J. G. D., 1932. The curved flint sickle blades of Britain. *Proceedings of the Prehistoric Society of East Anglia* 7, 67-81.

Clark, J. G. D., 1932. The date of the plano-convex flint-knife in England and Wales. *Antiquaries Journal* 12, 158-62.

Curwen, E. C., 1939. Blunted axe-like implements. *Proceedings of the Prehistoric Society* 5, 196-201.

Curwen, E. C., 1936. Non-crescentic sickle-flints from Sussex. *Antiquaries Journal* 16, 85-90.

Evans, J., 1897. *The Ancient Stone Implements, Weapons and Ornaments of Great Britain.* London.

Green, H. S., 1980. The flint arrowheads of the British Isles. *British Archaeological Reports* 75.
Grimes, W. F., 1931. The early bronze age flint dagger in England and Wales. *Proceedings of the Prehistoric Society of East Anglia* 6, 340-55.
Roe, F. E. S., 1979. Typology of stone implements with shaftholes. In T. H. McK. Clough and W. A. Cummins (eds), Stone Axe Studies, *Council for British Archaeology Research Report* no. 23, 23-48.
Smith, R. A., 1921. Hoards of neolithic celts. *Archaeologia* 71, 113-24.

Fieldwalking

Fasham, P. J., R. T. Shadla-Hall, S. J. Shennan and P. J. Bates, 1979. *Fieldwalking*. Hampshire County Council.

Index

Page numbers in bold type indicate where a term is defined. Those in italic refer to illustrations.

Adze 22, *23, 25, 26,* 37, *40*
Alternate flaking **22**
Archery *43,* 44
Arrowhead *18,* 19-21, 44, *47*
Artefact **51**
Assemblage **45, 51**
Association 38, 42
Axe 7, 9, 10, 11, 17, 22, *24, 25, 26, 27,* 31, 32, 33, *36,* 37, *40, 42*
Biface **11, 19,** 37
Blade *18,* **19,** 20, *21,* 38, 46
Blank **20,** 22, *23, 24,* 32
Brandon, Suffolk 6
Brittany 32, *36*
Bulb of force **20**
Burial 42, *43*
Butt **20**
Cache **32,** *34, 40*
Celt **22,** 22-4, *25,* 31, 32, *34, 36,* 42
Chalk 9, 10, 11
Chert 9, 16
Chronology 45, 49
Cissbury, W. Sussex 11
Collection **51**
Conchoidal fracture **7,** 9, 20
Core 11, *18,* **19,** 20, 28, 30, 46
Crested blade *18,* **19**
Curation **46**
Curwen, Cecil 38
Dagger 32, *36,* 49
Debitage **37**
Distribution 17, 31-6
Dorsal flake face **20**
Drilling 7, 25, *27,* 28, *29*
East Anglia 11, 16, 31
Easton Down, Wilts 11
Engineering, neolithic 10, 11
England 10, 38
Ethnography 37
European continent 17, 19, 32, *36*
Evans, Sir John 5, 38
Exchange 32, 35
Fieldwalking 50
Flake **7,** *18,* 19, 20, 21, 28, 30, *34, 35,* 37, 38, 44, *48,* 49
Flaking *6,* **7,** 9, 22, *26,* 28, *29*
Flint *4,* 7, 9, 10, 11, 16, 22, 30, 31, 38, 44, 46
Function of stone tools *see* Use
Grime's Graves, Norfolk *10,* 11, *30*
Grinding 22, 25, *26, 28, 29,* 49
Hammer, hard and soft *18,* **20**
Heat treatment of stone 30, 46
Hourglass perforation 25, *27*
Industry **51**
Ireland 9, 22, 32
Iron pyrites 44
Jade 17, 32, *36*
Knapping *see* Flaking
Langdale Pikes, Cumbria 9
Levallois core technique **28,** *30*
Manufacturing technology 19-30
Mercati 37
Mesolithic 9, *18,* 19, 20, 22, *23,* 25, *26, 27,* 31, *38,* 46, *48,* **51**
Microburin technique **20,** *21,* 37
Microwear analysis 38, *41*
Mine *4, 10,* 11, *12, 13, 14,* 15
Neolithic 9, 10, 11, *12-13, 18,* 19, 20, 22, *24, 25, 26, 27,* 30, 31, 38, 42, *43, 48,* 49, **51**
Nodule 10, 22

Pecking *6,* **7,** 9, 22, 24, 25, *27*
Penmaenmawr, Gwynedd 9, *28*
Perforation, techniques of 24-5, *27*
Petrology 8, 9, 16
'Pick', antler 11, *14*
Picrite, altered 31, *33*
Pitchstone *16,* 31, *33*
Platform, core **20**
Plot, Dr Robert 37
Preform **11,** 21, *25,* 32
Pressure-flaking 21, 30
Quarry *4,* 9, 31, 32
Retouch **20,** 37, *48,* 49
'Roughout' 11
Scafell Pikes, Cumbria 9
Scandinavia 32, *36*
Scotland *16,* 31
Scraper 37, *48*
Sickle gloss **38,** *40, 41*
Stone, properties of 7, 22
Stone, types of 7, 8
Stonehenge, Wilts 9, 44
Terminology 6
Thermoluminescence **46**
Tranchet blow **22,** *26*
Turned edge **21,** 22
Use of stone tools 37-44
Ventral flake face *18,* **20**
Wales 9, 32